CHESTER
A HISTORY

The Town Hall, Northgate Street, designed by W.H. Lynn of Belfast and built 1865-9. Watercolour with bodycolour over pencil by Louise Rayner (1832-1924).

CHESTER

A HISTORY

SIMON WARD

First published 2009 by Phillimore & Co Ltd
This edition 2013

The History Press
The Mill, Brimscombe Port
Stroud, Gloucestershire, GL5 2QG
www.thehistorypress.co.uk

British Library Cataloguing in Publication Data.
A catalogue record for this book is available from the British Library.

ISBN 978 0 7509 5553 9

Typesetting and origination by The History Press
Printed and bound in Great Britain by
Marston Book Services Limited, Oxfordshire

Contents

List of illustrations

Illustration Acknowledgements

The following illustrations are reproduced with kind permission:
Chester Archaeological Service, Chester City Council: 4, 5, 8, 9, 10, 11, 12, 13, 14, 15, 16, 18, 19, 20, 24, 25, 26, 29, 31, 33, 45, 47, 58, 59, 61, 62, 63, 66, 69, 71, 78, 83, 126, 148, 150. Chester History and Heritage, Chester City Council: 7, 40, 46, 49, 54, 56, 57, 75, 79, 80, 81, 85, 87, 96, 99, 101, 112, 113, 114, 116, 117, 120, 121, 122, 124, 128, 130, 132, 133, 135, 138, 139, 141, 142, 143, 144, 145. The Grosvenor Museum, Chester City Council: Frontispiece, 21, 22, 23, 28, 30, 32, 38, 41, 42, 44, 68, 72, 76, 102, 103, 104, 106, 107, 115, 118, 119, 127, 129, 131, 134.

Acknowledgements

This book could not have been written without the support, encouragement and editing skills, not to mention the Latin, of my wife Margaret. Over several centuries, a great number of books and papers have been written on the history of Chester and inevitably this book is built on the work of a large number of historians and scholars whose publications are gratefully acknowledged in the Notes. Foremost amongst these are the magisterial Chester volumes of the *Victoria County History* which have been recently published after many years of labour. I have also been able to draw upon the results of my own work on Chester's archaeology and on that of my colleagues in the Archaeological Service. Their knowledge and friendship have been a continual source of interesting and productive discussion and advice. I am grateful to be able to draw upon much of what has not yet been published. In particular, I wish to acknowledge the support of Mike Morris, City Archaeologist, and Mike Dix, Local Distinctiveness and Place Marketing Manager, for helping to provide the time and opportunity to write this book. Thanks are also due to Steve Woolfall, Heritage Services Manager, the staff at the Grosvenor Museum, particularly Peter Boughton, and at Chester History and Heritage, particularly Alison Watson, who have been an invaluable source of knowledge and illustrations.

Whilst acknowledging the contribution of these numerous sources, any inaccuracies remain the responsibility of the author. Inevitably, in a short history such as this, many incidents in the story have been omitted or glossed over, so I apologise if an aspect favoured by the reader is not well represented here. I have tried to weave together and describe those threads that I think have contributed most to the development and unique character of the city which has become my home.

Introduction

Chester is a famous and historic city. Indeed, it is famous for being historic. Each year it attracts millions of visitors who come to explore the historic sites, walk the walls and enjoy the exuberant architecture and discover the story behind the city. One of the great fascinations of Chester's story is the way that each age has contributed its own layer of evidence, changing but not entirely destroying what was there before. Moreover, this story is not yet fixed once and for all. Through the work of historians and archaeologists, new strands or forgotten threads are constantly coming to light. The subject has by no means become stale or exhausted.

Chester is in the North West, in the angle between Wales and England, at the south-eastern corner of the Irish Sea. It stands on a low hill, only about 100 feet high, overlooking the River Dee close to the former head of its estuary. The valley of the Dee is wide and low-lying and underlain by heavy boulder clay. The soil is, therefore, heavy and ill-drained and has historically not supported the most productive agriculture. Today it is mainly under pasture and is well known as dairy country. The low sandstone hills that protrude through the boulder clay have inevitably become the locations of the valley's settlements. On the eastern side, the valley is bounded by the mid-Cheshire ridge, a scarp once capped by the dense woods of Delamere Forest which has served to emphasise the historic separation of Chester from England. To the west and visible from most places in Chester are the hills of the Clwydian range, rough and disputed territory but rich in minerals and building stone. This physical setting has created the characteristic appearance and atmosphere of Chester, a walled city, on its low hill, surrounded by a flat plain. Buildings were constructed of red sandstone or timber-framing with slate roofs. Even after brick firing was introduced, the iron-rich boulder clay produced deep orange-red coloured buildings. The physical setting has also defined the politics and history of the city, its tradition of being distinct from England proper, and the relationship with Wales, competitive and sometimes hostile, but at the same time closely tied and economically interdependent.

1 *Aerial view of Chester from the south.*

The city defies easy categorisation. It is the county town of Cheshire but lies on its extreme western edge, only a mile or so from the border with Wales. It is in north-west England but looks across the border to north-east Wales for much of its business and contacts. It is at the mouth of the River Dee but nowadays has little to do with the sea. It has a long history and is full of ancient buildings but has one of the most vibrant property and business environments of the region. It is a small historic market town remote from the centres of power, but on occasion it has occupied the national stage and figured highly in military dispositions and the thoughts of monarchs. Over the centuries it has also given the impression of not quite living up to its potential, and yet it has a charm that has seduced many people, including the author, into settling and building their professional lives here.[1]

The first name that we have for Chester was the one given to it by the Romans – *Deva*, the place on the Dee. However, in Old Welsh it was known as *Caerlleon*, meaning 'the fortress-city of the legions'. This translated into Old English, the language of the Anglo-Saxons, as *Legacaestir*. In the 11th century the 'legion' element was dropped and the city became known as *Ceaster*, from which our modern Chester is directly derived. The -chester, -cester or -caster place-name element is a common one in English settlements with Roman antecedents, so in the later Middle Ages Chester was sometimes known as West Chester to distinguish it from those others.[2] The inhabitants of Chester are known as 'Cestrians'. The arms of the city, which have been in use from at least the 16th century, consist of the three gold lions of England halved with the three gold wheatsheaves of the Earl of Chester. The city's motto is 'Antiqui Colant Antiquum Dierum', which somewhat scrambled Latin is generally translated as 'Let the Ancients worship the Ancient of Days'. Historians have certainly followed this advice and Chester has been well studied over many years by numerous scholars.

The author first arrived in Chester in the early 1970s and has worked with the City Council's Archaeology Service ever since. At that time the city was emerging from a crisis of identity, a number of large developments having transformed the urban centre but also destroyed a significant portion of its heritage. There was a desire for a change of direction and the determination arose first to discover and then to preserve and protect the city's unique identity for posterity. It has been a privilege to have worked as part of and contributed to that movement.

2   *The motto and arms of Chester
on the Victorian Town Hall*

Chapter 1

Beginnings and the Arrival of the Romans

The River Dee flows in a circuitous course from Lake Bala in North Wales. At first, it heads south-eastwards, passing Llangollen in a steep gorge, before debouching onto the Cheshire Plain. In the flat, wide valley it adopts a sinuous, winding channel which turns northwards and has formed, for many centuries, the border between England and Wales. The river negotiates a few hills, outliers of the mid-Cheshire ridge, which have provided locations for settlement and crossing points (Farndon and Aldford). At the final hill, a broad, low sandstone ridge rising northwards, the Dee is forced to cut a looping gorge south-westwards then northwards before turning westwards to enter a long funnel-shaped estuary leading to the Irish Sea. Chester was built on this final hill in a position where it could overlook the estuary to the west and the river crossing to the south.

Recent archaeological discoveries have proved what has long been suspected: the Romans were not the first people to settle here. Under the Roman amphitheatre site are traces of Iron-Age round houses and ploughing dating from the second century B.C. and 'cord-rig' cultivation from just before the Roman conquest.[1] It appears therefore that the landscape was dotted with farmsteads and fields. The salt deposits and brine springs in central Cheshire were certainly being exploited by this time and salt was being traded around the coast and up the River Severn; the trade can be traced by the distribution of pottery containers for the salt.[2] However, Meols at the north-western tip of the Wirral peninsula, not Chester, was the main emporium at this time.

The Romans must have discovered the site of Chester by the late 50s, when the governor, Suetonius Paulinus, waged a campaign in North Wales. In A.D.60 he attacked and conquered Anglesey. During archaeological excavations in the city, traces of early ditches and wooden structures have been found beneath later Roman military buildings and these could be evidence for an auxiliary fort built to support the early campaigns.[3] The local Iron-Age tribe were the Cornovii and they seem to have acquiesced to Roman rule with little resistance, as did their neighbours in north-east Wales, the Deceangli, for the Romans were exploiting the lead resources on their territory by this time.

From the south Roman engineers built a straight road, an extension of Watling Street, which twice cut the winding course of the Dee, first at Aldford and then again at Chester. Then, in about A.D.74 or 75, a Roman legion, the II Adiutrix pia fidelis (second support legion, true and faithful), marched to Chester and established their legionary fortress. The II Adiutrix was a new legion that had been raised in A.D.69 by the Emperor Vespasian from marines of the fleet at Ravenna. It numbered about 6,000 armoured infantry who, like all Roman legionaries, were Roman citizens.

The arrival of the legion marks the foundation of Chester and the present city can be traced back directly to that time. As part of a renewed advance by the Roman army that would extend the empire into Scotland, Vespasian appointed a succession of three experienced military governors, Petillius Cerialis (71-4), Julius Frontinus (74-8) and Julius Agricola (78-84) to carry out this conquest and quell the turbulent tribes in the north of Britain. Three new legionary fortresses were established, at Chester, Caerleon in South Wales and York, which were really large permanent encampments that could house the legion plus all the headquarters, support facilities and stores that they required. These three bases, with Chester midway between the other two, were to form the backbone of the military dispositions in Roman Britain. Chester lay at the hub of a network of Roman roads. The main road south led to Wroxeter in Shropshire where it joined Watling Street, the road to London and the rest of the empire. A branch westwards from this road led into North Wales. The road eastwards headed to Manchester and across the Pennines to York. Another went north-eastwards towards the crossing of the Mersey at Wilderspool where it met the main road to the north. The road northwards from Chester was a local route running up the Wirral peninsula to Meols. To the west of the fortress lay the estuary, which soon developed as a port. The campaign in the north would have involved supply and perhaps landings by sea. The legion's marine origins were possibly one reason for their posting to Chester.

3 *The River Dee as it winds under the 14th-century bridge at Farndon.*

4 *Reconstruction of Deva in the first century.*

The fortress that Legio II Adiutrix built was named *Deva* after the British name for the River Dee. It had the traditional playing-card shape of Roman encampments, a rectangle with rounded corners. The north wall lay along the highest point of the hill where it overlooked the country beyond. The axis of the fortress was aligned on the main road from the south which entered via the south gate. It met the main east-west road at right angles outside the front of the *Principia* or headquarters building which occupied the centre of the fortress. This siting and planning of the fortress has had a profound effect on the subsequent development of Chester, for that road junction is now the Cross, the historic centre of the city. The main roads of the fortress became Eastgate Street, Watergate Street and Bridge Street.

The fortress was protected by a turf and earth rampart about ten feet or more tall and surmounted by a timber palisade. At each corner, and at intervals along the circuit, stood timber towers. There were four gates, also surmounted by timber towers, one in each of the sides. The north gate and east gate stood on the sites of their modern namesakes. The south gate lay at the bottom of Bridge Street and the west gate at the point where Watergate Street cuts Nicholas Street. Outside the rampart, the defences were completed by a ditch with a sharp V-shaped profile. Within the fortress, the majority of the buildings were constructed of timber and the remains of postholes set in slots dug in the ground are frequently found during excavations in the city.

The barracks of the soldiers were arranged in long blocks, each housing a century with the centurion's quarter at one end. The legion comprised ten cohorts, each of six centuries except for the first cohort, which had five double centuries. Most of the barracks were arranged around the periphery of the fortress, close to the defences. Their ovens and cookhouses were located immediately inside the rampart, safely distant from the wooden barracks across a wide road known as the 'intervallum road'.

The commander of the legion, the *legatus* or legate, had a large house on the east side of the headquarters building on the main east-west road, the *via principalis*. The barracks of the first cohort lay west of the headquarters. The centurion of the first century, the *primus pilus*, was the senior centurion in the legion. South of the *via principalis* lay the quarters of the tribunes, the senior officers under the legate. Both legate and tribunes were appointees from Rome who would serve in the army for a number of years during their careers in public office. Subsequently, they could hope to serve as consul at Rome and finally as governor of a province. The soldiers and centurions were professional soldiers who signed on for twenty years. At discharge they received a payment and grant of land.

Several of the buildings in the fortress were constructed of stone instead of timber, including the granaries, situated just inside the west gate close to the harbour. These substantial stone buildings with raised floors were designed to protect the legion's valuable food reserves from damp and fire. The bathhouse, adjacent to the south gate was another. The furnaces which heated the water and supplied the under-floor hypocaust systems obviously necessitated a stone structure. This was a magnificent building, with a colonnaded exercise hall and vaulted heated rooms.[4] It was not just a washing facility for the soldiers but more like a modern leisure centre where the soldiers could exercise and spend their free time.

From its foundation, the fortress at Chester was unusually large. Most legionary fortresses were about fifty acres in size; Chester was sixty acres. It is now clear that the extra space was allocated to a group of special buildings which occupied a block in the centre of the fortress behind the *principia*. The most striking of these was the stone building comprising a tall elliptical structure with twelve radiating rooms set around an open courtyard. In the centre was a monument incorporating a fountain. The elliptical structure was set within a rectangular block which included a small bathhouse on its southern side. The building is unique in the Roman world. It has been studied by Dr D. Mason who suggests that it was designed as an *imago mundi*, a monument to display and celebrate the Roman world view.[5] The twelve rooms could have been dedicated to major events in Rome's history, to different parts of the empire or to the principal gods of the Roman pantheon. Another building occupying this central space was a large courtyard structure, with offices or storerooms surrounding a central space in which stood a rectangular hall-like building.[6] These special buildings possibly comprised an imperial governor's quarter set safely within the defences of the legionary fortress.[7] From here, in the centre of the military forces that he commanded,

5 *Post-holes and slots from first-century timber centurions quarter on the Northgate Brewery site, 1974.*

the governor could control the conquest of the rest of Britain. We know that the governor Agricola even contemplated the invasion of Ireland for which, of course, Chester would have been ideally sited. But the elliptical building and the courtyard building were not completed, even though the foundations were built and lead water pipes laid. The pipes are important evidence because they were stamped with the name of the governor, Julius Agricola, and can be dated to A.D.79. Work must have stopped shortly after and other building plots in this area were also left vacant. The army was heavily engaged in Scotland by this time and when the campaigns had quietened down priorities had changed and the proposed governor's quarter was no longer required.

6 *Columns from the bathhouse which were discovered in the 19th century. They have been re-erected in the Roman Gardens.*

The presence of several thousand soldiers and a large military installation inevitably attracted a settlement of civilians around the fortress, known as *canabae*. The extent of the civilian development at this early stage is not clear because the earliest levels are obscured beneath later activity but it is certain that the military would have kept a close eye on it. The main road eastwards, now Foregate Street, was probably occupied by long timber strip buildings which had shops or other commercial activity at the end fronting the street and living quarters at the back. There were official buildings in the *canabae* too. Adjacent to the east gate, on the north side, a large area was kept open to serve as the parade ground. On the south side, adjacent to the road which crossed the river, a building identified as a *mansio* or posting inn has been found.[8] This would have served officials travelling on the Emperor's business as well as ordinary travellers. Another major structure built at this early stage was the first amphitheatre, which lay outside the south-eastern corner of the fortress. It is now known that it was another of the structures built in stone from the first and would have been an impressive and iconic symbol of Roman culture.[9]

Beyond the settled area lay the cemeteries. A remarkable collection of tombstones survives from the Roman period and is now kept in the Grosvenor Museum.[10] Many were later built into the city walls and so preserved. Several record soldiers from the

7 *Lead pipe stamped with the names of the emperor, Vespasian, and the governor, Agricola, and dated to A.D.79. It was found in Eastgate Street in 1899.*

Second Legion who had died in service. They were born in towns in Thrace, Dalmatia and Pannonia (Roman provinces now largely in the countries of the former Yugoslavia or western Turkey). One named Crispus was a veteran who had completed his term of service. Perhaps he chose to settle near his old comrades or he may have been retained in special employment by the army. These tombstones show how diverse the population of Roman Chester was, particularly in its early days.

A revolt in Dacia on the empire's border along the River Danube brought the first chapter in Chester's history to an end. Reinforcements were urgently required so the Second Legion Adiutrix together with a number of auxiliary units were withdrawn from Britain around 88-90 for service on the Danube frontier. This necessitated a major redeployment of the Roman forces in Britain and a withdrawal from Highland Scotland. The legion stationed in Scotland, Legio XX Valeria Victrix, abandoned its partly constructed fortress at Inchtuthil in Perthshire and possibly returned for a short while to its old fortress at Wroxeter before being moved forward to Chester around A.D.90.

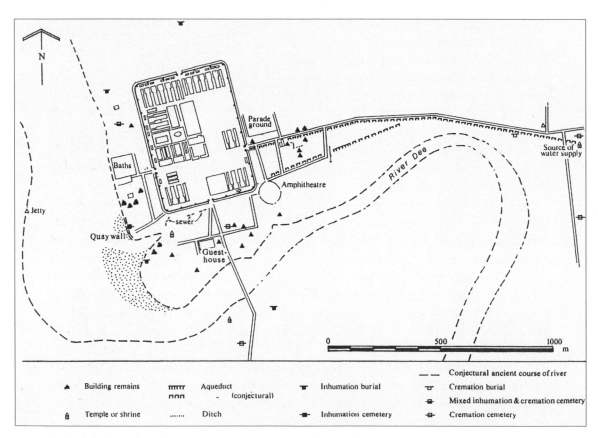

8 *Plan of Roman Chester.*

Chapter 2

In Imperial Rome, the Legion and Civilians

T he 20th Legion which arrived at Chester in about A.D.90 formed the garrison for the next two centuries or so. Legio XX Valeria Victrix was a long-established unit that had taken part in the Roman invasion of Britain in A.D.43. It was first stationed in Colchester but had moved to Gloucester and then to Wroxeter to participate in the conquest of Wales. It earned its title 'Victrix' during the battle against Boudicca in 60. It joined the campaign in the north of Britain, but following the retirement from Scotland was stationed in the vacant fortress of Chester. Almost immediately a major programme of rebuilding was initiated which extended into the second century. The Roman army was not just a well trained and efficiently organised fighting force. It included in its numbers the engineers, surveyors, builders and craftsmen that it needed to construct the roads and forts it used and to manufacture much of its equipment.

Many of the timber buildings were rebuilt in stone including the *principia* (headquarters building). The rear part of the *principia* comprised an impressive aisled hall or basilica.[1] Parts of the sandstone columns can still be seen in the cellar of a shop in Northgate Street. A range of rooms ran behind the hall, the central one of which formed the shrine in which the eagle and other standards of the legion were stored. A basement below the shrine contained the strong room where the legion's pay chest and other funds were kept secure. It was discovered during redevelopment in the 1960s.[2]

Another major project undertaken from about A.D.100 was the enhancement of the defences by the addition of a sandstone facing to the front of the turf rampart. This was no ordinary revetment wall but an extremely impressive, finely built, masonry construction using huge squared blocks of sandstone, some over a yard long. At parapet level, there was a projecting decorative cornice. The rampart was built up against the back of the wall to form a new wall walk. Long sections of this wall have stood the test of time and may still be observed today.[3] The gates and towers were rebuilt in stone as well. A fragment of an inscription, found in 1884 in the Kaleyards area (outside the walls), finely carved on a slate slab, may have come from the East Gate. It has been interpreted as including the name of the Emperor Trajan (A.D.98-117)

9 *Column bases of the* Principia *and columns lying where they fell, as discovered in the cellar of 23 Northgate Street.*

and so is further evidence for the date of the wall's construction.[4] The sandstone for all the building work was quarried from the immediate area of the fortress. Roman quarries lay outside the North Gate and on both banks of the river where it cuts through the ridge which Chester occupies. In Handbridge, on the south side of the river, a relief carving of the goddess Minerva cut into the surviving quarry face has long been known. Minerva was patron, amongst other things, of craftsmen and so particularly appropriate for watching over the quarrymen. The legion also established a works-depot at Holt, about seven miles up the Dee from Chester, where roof and hypocaust tiles and pottery were manufactured. Roof tiles stamped with 'LEG XX VV', the mark of the legion, are a common find in Chester. Some of the new building, however, continued to be in timber, particularly some of the barracks.[5] They were presumably a lower priority for reconstruction in stone.

The economic stimulation provided by a large establishment of troops for several decades is evidenced by the expansion of the *canabae*, or civil settlement

10 *The strong room at the rear of the* Principia, *excavated in 1969 and still preserved beneath the Council Offices.*

11   *Roman masonry surviving up to cornice level in the north City Wall.*

12   *Foundations of the south-eastern angle tower. At this point the Roman wall lay forward of the line of the later medieval wall.*

13 *The shrine of Minerva carved in the quarry face in Handbridge.*

around the fortress, in the early second century. The part to the east, along Foregate Street, remained the main commercial area with some industrial activity as well. Traces of metalworking and pottery making have been found during modern development in this area. To the west, between the fortress and the harbour, there were more elaborate buildings. Some close to the river were masonry and may have been secure warehousing adjacent to the port. Others were of timber but comprised more elaborate accommodation than those in the area east of the fortress, with painted plaster on their walls and raised timber floors. Initially, they may have been provided for officials of the imperial administration or possibly foreign merchants. In this area, another substantial bathhouse was built, complementing the existing one inside the fortress. Such a complex classical structure must have been built by the military and was perhaps used by them as well, providing a more relaxed facility outside the constraints of the fortress, but was no doubt used by civilians as well, encouraging them to adopt Roman culture.

14 *The excavation of a first cohort centurion's quarter, with painted wall plaster and mortar floors still surviving, at the Crook Street site, 1974.*

15 *A battery of bread ovens in a rampart building, Abbey Green site, 1976.*

16 *Stone-built houses in the civil settlement, Priory Place site, 1989.*

17 *The main entrance into the arena of the Roman amphitheatre.*

Entertainment was also provided by the amphitheatre which was refurbished at this time. The existing earth seating bank was partly dug away and replaced by seating raised on a wooden substructure. New access stairs were built against the outside wall. This converted the amphitheatre into one of the so-called 'Pompeian-type', an unusually elaborate form for so remote a location. The arena floor was also lowered. The new seating bank and deeper arena improved the view of the spectacles. The entertainments provided probably included beast hunts and fights and perhaps even gladiatorial combats. Recent excavations on the site have revealed the range of activities that went on immediately around the amphitheatre.[6] Just by the main north entrance was a shrine, possibly the original location of the Nemesis altar dedicated to the goddess of fate or retribution. There were also latrine pits, the posts for stalls from which food snacks or even souvenirs could be bought, and evidence for dogs scavenging through the refuse – just the sort of activities that might be found around a modern sporting venue.

The period of building and activity suffered a temporary decline in the second century. In A.D.120 the Emperor Hadrian decided to build a wall to form a secure northern boundary to the empire. All the legions in Britain, including the Twentieth, were heavily engaged in its construction and garrisoning. However, their legionary fortress at Chester was not abandoned. It served as a supply and service base for the work in the north and no doubt retained the administrative staff and a skeleton

18   *Excavation of the north-western seating bank of the Roman amphitheatre, 2005.*

garrison. It was well placed to send supplies north by sea to Carlisle at the western end of the wall. The occupation of Hadrian's Wall was followed in A.D.140 by the reoccupation of southern Scotland and the construction of the Antonine Wall across the Forth-Clyde isthmus. The Chester fortress must have had a rather dilapidated air during this period. Barracks in the Northgate area had been demolished and were not rebuilt. In the central area, the elliptical building site and adjacent blocks were left open and used for rubbish dumping. The civil settlement around the fortress probably also suffered from the absence of soldiers and their spending power, although it was gaining an economic life of its own independently of the military presence and the evidence for decline is not so marked. The possible official residences to the west of the fortress were demolished and replaced by stone buildings on a completely different layout. They had much more diverse plans but still provided a high standard of accommodation, boasting painted walls and hypocaust heating systems. A Roman cemetery found under the old Royal Infirmary north of this area may have served this community.[7] Interestingly, the *mansio* or official inn on the road south from the fortress was another building left incomplete at this time.[8]

In the late second century, the garrison of Deva gradually returned to close to its full complement. Southern Scotland was abandoned in the 160s and Hadrian's Wall recommissioned. However, troops from the legion were retained in the north

19 *The 'tethering stone' placed in the centre of the arena. The lead plug which held the iron loop can be seen.*

to garrison Corbridge, Carlisle and Newstead. At the death of the emperor Commodus in A.D.192 civil war swept the empire. The British governor, Clodius Albinus, rebelled and led his army, including parts of the Twentieth, to Gaul. He was defeated near Lugdunum by the new emperor Septimius Severus and no doubt the legion suffered significant losses. Further unrest in Britain was quelled by the Severus' campaign in Scotland in 208-11. The return to a near full garrison necessitated another major programme of rebuilding. In the decades around A.D.200 practically every building in the fortress was repaired or reconstructed. The defensive walls were either completed (if they had not been previously) or significantly repaired. A section of the east wall may even have fallen down.[9] Those buildings that had not previously been completed were finished for the first time, including the enigmatic elliptical building. Even though the site had been abandoned to rubbish dumping from the nearby workshops, and the stubs of the walls had been long buried, the plans were resurrected. The completed building was similar but not exactly identical to the original uncompleted design. Its function remains as mysterious as before. The great bathhouse was also reconstructed with new hypocausts installed and the bathing provision rearranged. The fortress of Deva was only now completed to something like its intended design.

An important political development in A.D.212, the 'constitutio Antoniniana', must have had a significant effect on the people of Chester. Roman citizenship was extended to all freeborn people. Also, soldiers' conditions were improved and they were allowed to marry during their service and not just on discharge. This regularised those liaisons which must have been going on and secured inheritance rights for widows and children. A probable consequence of this was the erosion of the distinction between fortress and civil settlement. In the long term, too, it diminished the mobility of the legions. The third century was a time of prosperity for Chester. More substantial stone buildings are known within the civil settlement. Plots of land that had been left vacant in the western area were now filled in. These new buildings included several with hypocaust heating systems and fine painted walls.

Major reconstruction work occurred at the amphitheatre. A new external wall was built enclosing the old structure and greatly increasing its seating capacity. Eight new spectator entrances were incorporated into it, leading directly up into the seating banks, separate from the main entrances into the arena. The outer façade was embellished with engaged columns. In the centre of the arena was placed a massive sandstone block with an iron hoop set in it to which human or animal victims could be chained. It prevented them from seeking shelter against the arena wall and spoiling the view for the spectators.[10]

A remarkable collection of altars and tombstones has survived from the third century because they were subsequently used to repair the fortress wall. They record some of the names, the lives and beliefs of both soldiers and civilians living in Chester. Many fine tombstones were set up to civilians and show that the settlement prospered through that time.[11] Stones showing a banquet scene with the deceased lying on a couch seem to have been popular. Notable are ones recording only women, such as Curatia Dinysia (perhaps a misspelling of Dionysia), whose heir set up the stone. Another commemorates the centurion Marcus Aurelius Nepos and his wife, who set up the stone. Both are represented in the carving, but no one added her inscription following her death so the space is left blank and she remains anonymous. One interesting stone, found in 1874, was apparently still *in situ* above a grave containing two skeletons which was dug close to the then bank of the River Dee on the Roodee. The stone records Callimorphus (aged 42) and Serapion (aged three and a half). It was set up by Theseus to his brother and son. It is not certain from the inscription

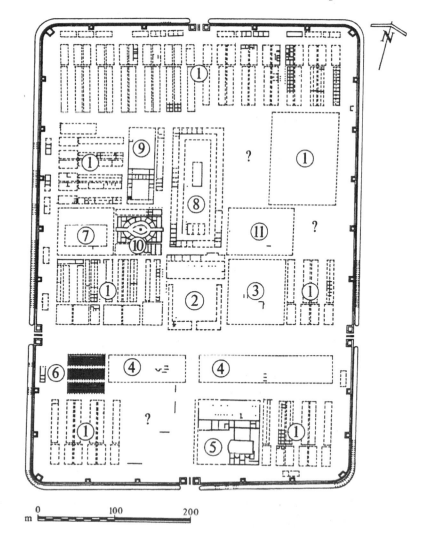

20 *Plan of the Roman fortress:*

1 *barracks*
2 *Principia*
3 *Commander's House*
4 *senior officers*
5 *bathhouse*
6 *granaries*
7 *workshops*
8 *stores compound or hospital*
9 *stores compound*
10 *elliptical building*
11 *alternative site for hospital*

21   *Tombstone of Curatia Dinysia, showing her reclining on a banqueting couch.*

whether Serapion was the son of Callimorphus or Theseus. These are names of Greek origin and, given the location of the grave and design of the tombstone, they are thought to belong to civilians, perhaps merchants from the eastern Mediterranean. Another stone with maritime connections commemorates an unnamed *optio* or junior officer. The stone is broken and the name was carved on the missing upper portion. The officer died in a shipwreck. The standard formula at the base of the stone, 'H S E' (*hic situs est* – here lies), is here represented just by 'S E' as, presumably, the burial place was not known. Amphorae, the large pottery containers which carried bulk goods around the Mediterranean, are commonly found in Chester and are further evidence for maritime trade. They show that wine, olive oil and fish sauce were shipped to Chester.

An important development in the third century was the provision of defences for the civilian town. On the west a clay bank was built over the former stone warehouse buildings. However, a far more impressive monument, still partly visible to this day, is the so-called 'quay wall'. This massive structure bounds the western side of the settlement along the riverfront. Founded on the river bed, it revetted the tall bank of the river to a height exceeding 30 feet. It is familiarly known as the 'quay wall' but that function can be doubted on the grounds both of practicality and of its monumentality. A defensive wall to protect the smart houses and the bathhouse in this area was perhaps a more likely reason for building.[12] Ditches on the eastern side of the town could be part of a less elaborate circuit on that side.

The civilian settlement must also have contained temples though the buildings themselves have not been found. A fragmentary inscription from a rubbish dump on the eastern side of the town refers to a temple. The funerary monuments and altars indicate that the pantheon of Roman gods

22   *Tombstone of the centurion Marcus Aurelius Nepos and his wife. The inscription recording her name was never added.*

and the spirits of the emperors were revered. Sculpture fragments show that the cult of Mithras was practised.

Modern development around Chester has produced archaeological evidence for extensive activity in the immediate hinterland. Some of this area would have remained under the direct control of the legion in order to supply produce and provide grazing for its animals. However, the settlement at Heronbridge, on the main road just to the south of Chester, was probably outside military control. Physically separated from the town by the river and open countryside, it originated at the end of the first century and continued to grow through the second century with the erection of substantial stone buildings. Impressive funerary monuments were built there, too, overlooking the river.[13] Similar settlements, close to but separate from legionary fortresses, are known elsewhere in the Roman Empire. They probably had the advantage of proximity to the economic prosperity generated by the presence of the army but were not under military control like the civil settlement around the fortress was. On the outskirts of the settlements at Chester and Heronbridge, we now know that the landscape was farmed and featured fields and droveways and perhaps small settlements like the one at Saltney overlooking the Dee estuary.[14]

Aerial photography has revealed at least a dozen practice camps in an arc about two to three miles east and north-east of Chester. They were built on the heathland that once characterised this area. The camps are small, rectangular, ditched enclosures – in effect a mini-Roman fort. One can imagine a small body of soldiers being sent out to construct one and perhaps camp there for a short time to keep their field skills up to scratch during periods when they were not on active campaign.

Although this was in many ways the heyday of Roman Chester, significant changes were under way in the later part of the third century. The legion was reduced in size to possibly fewer than a thousand men. Detachments of troops were sent periodically to support the armies on the Rhine and Danube and it is likely

23 *Tombstone of Callimorphus and Serapion found above their grave on the Roodee. Their names are Greek.*

that many did not return. Cavalry became a more important element of the army and tombstones of cavalrymen have been found in Chester.[15] One striking example portrays a Sarmatian holding a dragon standard. The Sarmatians came from the area of the lower Danube and were recruited into the Roman army. In A.D.175, a force of 5,500 had been sent to Britain by the Emperor Marcus Aurelius.

The later history of the Twentieth Legion and Roman Chester is obscure. We do not know quite what became of the bustling and prosperous town of the third century. Finds of pottery and coins show that the fortress and civil town continued

24 *The so-called Roman Quay Wall on the Roodee, marking the former bank of the river.*

to be occupied through to the late fourth century. Many of the major buildings were repaired and maintained through this time, including the *principia*, the bathhouses, barracks and the *mansio*.[16] The *mansio* had suffered a catastrophic fire at the end of the third century, the skeleton of one unfortunate victim being found down its well. The young man was lame as he had a badly healed fracture of his lower leg. We do not know whether he had jumped into the well to escape the flames or if he was unceremoniously dumped down it afterwards when the site was cleared. Masses of burnt building debris including masonry and painted wall plaster were thrown down the well when the site was cleared for rebuilding.[17]

In the fourth century the Roman emperors adopted Christianity so it is likely that there were churches in Chester, but they have yet to be found. Major repair work was carried out on the defensive walls. It was possibly at this time that the old tombstones were gathered together and reused in the core of the wall.[18] Numerous barbarian invasions across the Danube and Rhine together with revolts by the governors of Britain are likely to have depleted the garrison. The latest evidence for the Twentieth Legion's actually being at Chester is some roof tiles bearing its stamp dating to A.D.249-51, and the latest evidence for the legion's existence is on the coinage of the usurper Carausius in 289-90.[19] But a military presence continued well into the fourth century and coins occur up to the 380s. Pottery from the late fourth and early fifth centuries, including imports from the Mediterranean, has been found although in small amounts. It is still one of the great puzzles of archaeology why and how the thriving towns of Roman Britain had practically disappeared by the fifth century. In Chester, perhaps the removal of the garrison and imperial officials and the disruption of trade and economic activity due to barbarian invasions all contributed to the decline. The need and ability of the settlement to support a large population had simply disappeared.

Chapter 3

Britons, Saxons and Vikings – Heroes, Legends and Saints

After the end of the Roman period the population of Chester collapsed, and the story of the next few centuries is one put together from myth and legend but scant hard evidence. The decline was partly due to the political and economic changes that marked the abandonment of Britain by the Roman Empire. Outbreaks of plague in the sixth century may also have disrupted urban life. However, Chester did not entirely disappear. There were still massive remains of the Roman military buildings, particularly the walls and gates, the bathhouses, the *principia* and the amphitheatre. There must have been people as well. A handful of fifth- and sixth-century pottery sherds shows that a small amount of trade with the Mediterranean continued. The inhabitants may well have found the civil settlement east of the fortress more comfortable for a reduced population than the massive classical buildings in the fortress.

The Chester area passed under the control of Powys, the minor British kingdom of north-east Wales. The inhabitants were apparently Christian by this time as the names of two nearby villages, Christleton (settlement of Christians) and Eccleston (settlement with a church), show. At Bangor-on-Dee there was an important monastery with, reputedly, thousands of monks. In this murky period, two historical events stand out: the synod of Chester in 603 and the battle of Chester in 616. The synod probably held at Chester was attended by St Augustine and major figures from the British church, including the monks from Bangor-on-Dee, in order to determine whether the Celtic or the Roman tradition should be followed. The British decided to hold to their traditions but were warned that dire consequences would follow.

In 616 King Aethelfrith of Northumbria launched an attack on the King of Gwynedd, who was sheltering Edwin, a claimant for his throne. A hastily gathered British army met the Northumbrians at Chester but were defeated with a great slaughter. The British were supported by the monks from Bangor-on-Dee and Bede says that 1,200 were killed in the battle, thus confirming St Augustine's prophecy.[1] In 1930 a battle cemetery was discovered at Heronbridge, south of Chester, overlying the Roman settlement there. It was situated within a large earthwork enclosure set between the River Dee and the Roman road, and was recently relocated in excavations by Chester Archaeological Society.[2] The skeletons were packed together in a pit which is estimated to contain well over 100 bodies. Two were lifted for detailed analysis. They had clearly died from savage sword cuts to the head and radiocarbon samples established their early seventh-century date. It seems certain that these are casualties of the battle and mark the site of the encounter. The excavations also proved that the earthwork was of a similar date and was possibly thrown up to protect the Northumbrians' camp.[3] Aethelfrith did not long enjoy the fruits of victory; he was killed shortly after and Edwin took his throne.

By the late seventh century, as Saxon power gradually spread westwards, Chester was absorbed into the Saxon kingdom of Mercia whose power base lay in the Midlands. The church of St John the Baptist was reputedly founded by King Aethelred in 689. It lay outside the Roman fortress near the amphitheatre. This area south-east of the Roman centre was the focus of the Mercian town. Another major church, dedicated to St Peter and St Paul, was founded within the Roman fortress. The archaeological evidence for the period is scant, comprising an occasional find and plough soils over

25 *Post-holes of Dark-Age timber buildings erected in the amphitheatre arena.*

Roman remains.[4] Timber buildings were erected in the arena of the amphitheatre and the entrances were blocked but the dating of this is unclear.[5] Near the Cross, a stone building, possibly also of this period, has been found,[6] but the major Roman buildings must have become increasingly derelict and dangerous. The collapsed columns of the hall of the headquarters can still be seen in the cellar of a shop in Northgate Street. At the great bathhouse, the tiled vault over the heated rooms was found lying where it fell, sealing a deposit of dark earth 10 inches thick which had accumulated on the slate slab floor. This deposit indicates some sort of occupation after the baths ceased to function but before the roof collapsed.[7]

Towards the end of the ninth century the situation of Chester changed dramatically. Former Viking raids had led to the conquest and settlement of the whole north and east of England. The eastern half of Mercia was lost to the Danelaw. Only Wessex under its king, Alfred the Great, held out, although sorely pressed. Chester was the most north-westerly town remaining in Saxon hands. Moreover, it lay on the route between the major Viking centres of Dublin and York. In 893 a Danish army occupied 'waste' or 'deserted' Chester and were besieged by the Saxons for two days. Then, in 903, the Vikings were expelled from Dublin and a group of Norsemen led

26 *The shattered remains of the front face of the Roman fortress wall where it had fallen outwards, St John Street site, 1987.*

by Ingimund arrived in Wirral just north of Chester.[8] They were granted land to settle by Aethelred, the ealdorman of Mercia, and his wife Aethelflaed. Aethelflaed was the daughter of King Alfred and the power behind the throne in Mercia. Alfred had died and Wessex was ruled by Aethelflaed's brother, Edward the Elder. Ingimund apparently tried to seize Chester but was forestalled by the Saxon army. In consequence, in 907 Aethelflaed established a *burh* or defended settlement at Chester. The system of *burhs* had been introduced to Wessex by King Alfred and was a remarkably successful strategy in halting the Viking expansion. The local inhabitants were given the responsibility of maintaining the *burh*'s defences which then provided them with a refuge in time of Viking attack. Alfred's successors extended the system into Mercia. The more successful *burhs*, like Chester, developed into centres of administration,

27 *Tenth-century Saxon cross head found at St John's church.*

justice, coinage and commerce. The foundation of the *burh* led to the full reoccupation of the old Roman fortress.

Aethelflaed is closely associated with another Saxon woman, Chester's patron saint, St Werburgh. Ironically, Werburgh never visited the city during her lifetime. She was a seventh-century Mercian princess who became a nun and rose to be in charge of all the nunneries in Mercia. She was noted for her piety and after her death in about A.D.700 miraculous tales of her sanctity accumulated. Most famous (although mythical) is the story of the geese. Flocks of wild geese had been causing depredations to the fields of the nunnery estates at Weedon, Northamptonshire. When informed of this, Werburgh instructed her servant to lock the geese in the church for the night. To the servant's surprise, the geese acquiesced.

The following morning, Werburgh instructed the geese to leave the fields alone and let them out to fly away. Instead of flying off, however, they circled the church honking in distress for one of their number was missing. Werburgh ascertained that the goose had in fact been roasted and eaten. She was presented with the carcass and miraculously restored it to life. It flew off and joined its brothers in the sky. Needless to

28 *Silver pennies of King Athelstan (924-39) minted at Chester, the left one by the moneyer Eadmund and the right one by Maeldomen.*

say, the geese never committed damage to the crops in Weedon again. After her death, Werburgh was buried in Hanbury, Staffordshire.

Her relics were subsequently translated to Chester. There are various stories about how this happened and a little skulduggery may have been involved. Ranulf Higden, a monk of Chester writing around 1352, records the tradition that in 875 the nuns of Hanbury, fearing the proximity of the Danes, removed their precious relics to Chester for greater safety and deposited them at the church of Saints Peter and Paul. Another theory involves Aethelflaed. According to Henry Bradshaw (a monk who died in 1513), at the same time as Aethelflaed founded the *burh* in 907, she refounded the church of Saints Peter and Paul as a college of secular canons dedicated to St Werburgh and moved the saint's relics there. Burh, church, saint's shrine and mint were thus all part of the same military and political message, and ensured that Chester remained firmly within the Saxon orbit. Is Higden's story of the 875 translation, therefore, a bit of 'spin' designed to make Chester's acquisition of the relics rather more respectable?

Another saint with close connections to Chester was Plegmund. He is supposed to have lived as a hermit on an island in the River Gowy at Plemstall near Mickle Trafford, close to Chester, although a hermit's life does not quite fit in with his later career.[9] He was renowned as a scholar and was summoned to the court of King Alfred. In 890 he was appointed Archbishop of Canterbury and in that capacity crowned Edward the Elder. Plegmund died in 923 and was canonised. St Plegmund's Well may still be seen on the outskirts of Mickle Trafford close to St Peter's church, which is reputed to stand on the site of the saint's retreat.[10]

Aethelflaed is also credited with founding the church of St Peter, at the Cross. She died in 918 and King Edward incorporated the remains of Mercia into his kingdom. He died in 924 at Farndon, south of Chester, and in 937 King Athelstan

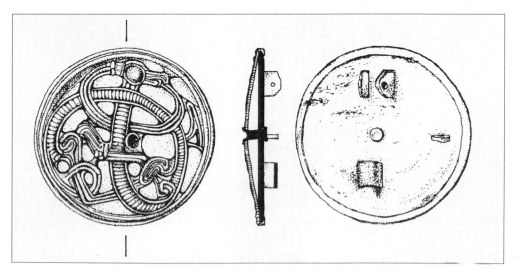

29   *Copper alloy disc brooch with interlaced animal design. It is in Viking style and was possibly made in Dublin.*

30 *Part of the Castle Esplanade hoard found in 1950. It contained coins, silver ingots and hacsilber (pieces chopped up for resmelting), and was buried in a Chester Ware cooking pot in the 970s.*

won a major battle over the Norse and Scots at 'Brunanburh', which is thought to be modern Bromborough, a short distance north of Chester.

Chester prospered in the tenth century, benefiting from its access to the Irish Sea and its trading contacts with the Welsh and particularly the Vikings. It had a very mixed Anglo-Saxon and Norse or Hiberno-Norse population. The mint at Chester produced silver pennies and most of the moneyers were Scandinavian. For a while, under Athelstan, it was the most prolific mint in the country. It is thought that the Scandinavians concentrated in the Lower Bridge Street area towards the river, whilst the Saxons or English occupied the old Roman fortress area. Two further churches were probably founded in this period in the southern part of the city, those of St Bridget and St Olave. The former is dedicated to an Irish saint and the latter is the patron saint of Norway who died in 1030, so both indicate Viking influence.

At this time, the houses were wooden, and numerous examples have been found in excavations across the city.[11] A variety of styles is present in both Saxon and Scandinavian traditions. Saxon styles comprise 'halls' built at ground level and 'sunken

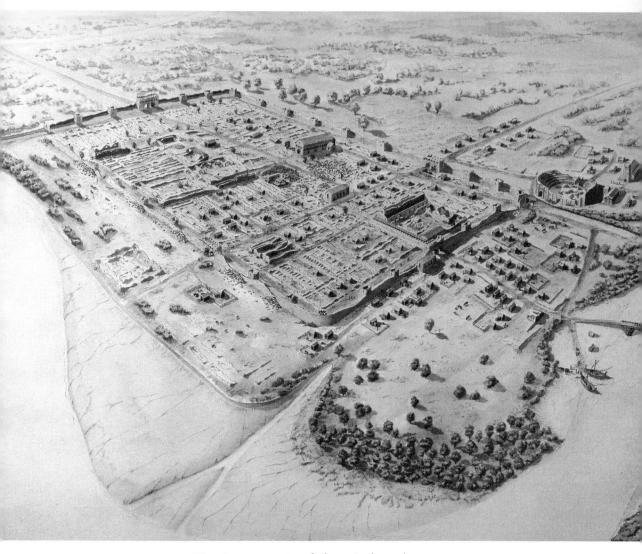

31   *A reconstruction of Chester in the tenth century.*

featured buildings' with floor areas set below the ground. There are also Viking-style semi-basemented buildings where the basements are set partly below ground with an upper floor above.[12] One characteristic of the city's layout was the way in which the buildings were spread across the occupied area with open ground between them. They were not concentrated on the street frontages as happened later. It was probably at this time that many of the ruined Roman buildings were cleared and the southern end of Northgate Street was driven through to the Cross. Of other major buildings that must have existed, such as a moot or common hall and residences for royal officials, we have no knowledge. Pottery came into widespread use again, although so-called Chester Ware was probably made in Stafford and elsewhere and just traded to Chester. Evidence for Viking trade is the discovery of Chester Ware in Dublin and even Trondheim.[13] Trade was obviously two-way, as is shown by a Viking copper-alloy disc brooch found at the Hunter Street School site in 1981 which is virtually identical to one from Dublin and was probably made there.[14] Antler working is another craft for which archaeological evidence has emerged.[15]

Chester remained an important military and naval base during the Saxon period. In 973 King Edgar came to Chester with his navy and was rowed on the Dee to St John's by perhaps eight (the sources vary) Scots, Viking and Welsh princes in an act of submission.[16] The prosperity and stability of the tenth century did not last, however, and was ended by the wars between Ethelred II and the Kings of Denmark. The output of the mint declined and in 980 the city was raided by the Vikings. Several large coin hoards from the period reflect this instability. In 1016 Edmund Ironside ravaged the city because it would not come out to fight the Danes. The loyalty of its Anglo-Scandinavian population was perhaps viewed with suspicion. In the 11th century, under Kings Cnut and Edward the Confessor, more settled times returned and trade recovered somewhat. It was certainly well organised by 1066, as is recorded in Domesday Book, but loss of lands in north-east Wales to the Welsh and the rise of Bristol probably affected the city adversely. At this time the earldormen or earls of Mercia became more significant figures again. Earl Leofric (d. 1057) is best remembered as the husband of Lady Godiva, but in Chester he was a great benefactor of St Werburgh's and St John's. He gave them money and lands and beautified their churches. By 1066 Earl Edwin had become one of the largest landholders in the city.

Chapter 4
The Walled City

Chester is justly famous for its city walls and the modern visitor to the city is welcomed to 'The Walled City'. In the past, of course, being enclosed by city walls was not an unusual attribute for a town, particularly one lying close to what were regarded as the more turbulent parts of the country.[1] Chester stands out, however, because it has retained its circuit of walls almost complete down to the present day.

In A.D.907, during the reconquest of Mercia from the Scandinavians by the Saxon kings of Wessex, Chester was refounded as a *burh*, and the Domesday Survey entry for Chester throws light on the way the maintenance of the burghal defences was organised. It records that: 'For the repair of the city wall and bridge the reeve used to call out one man to come from each hide in the county.'[2] Although the Survey dates to nearly two centuries after the foundation, this entry sounds very similar to the arrangements put in place in Wessex to maintain and defend burh walls, and is thought to record the arrangement established by Aethelflaed at Chester. Under King Alfred each hide was required to provide one man to defend the walls and four men were required to cover each 'pole'.[3] Chester's assessment at 1,200 hides corresponds with the 12 hundreds into which the ancient county of Cheshire was divided.

We do not know the line of the burghal defences at Chester but we do have some good pointers and we can make some informed guesses. It presumably formed an intermediate stage between the Roman circuit, which we do know, and the medieval line which survives today. In 907 the Roman walls must have still been standing to a considerable degree since substantial lengths survive to this day, incorporated into the existing fabric. The modern walls follow the Roman line on the east and north but have been extended outwards on the southern and western sides as far as the ancient bank of the River Dee. The Saxon defences, therefore, would also have incorporated the Roman northern and eastern defences. Along many stretches, this would have consisted of the impressive masonry curtain wall and earth rampart. The Roman North Gate and East Gate may well have survived too. It is a curious fact, however, that at the location of each interval tower, the Roman wall does not survive. It appears

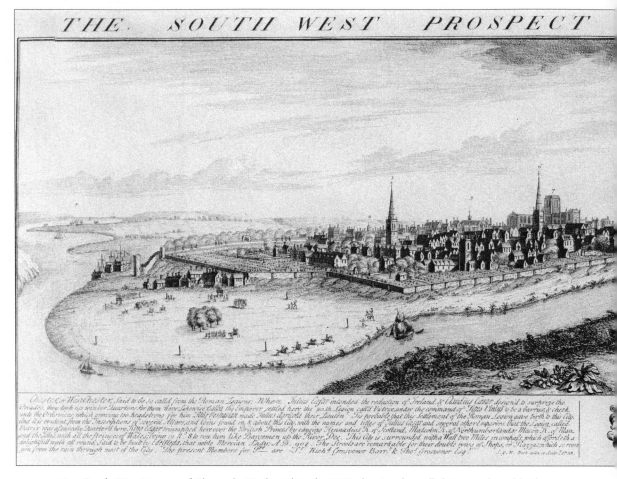

32 *South West Prospect of Chester by Nathaniel Buck, 1728, showing the walled city, castle and bridge.*

that where it was backed by the turf and earth rampart, the masonry could subside back against it and so remain standing. Where the towers stood the wall was too rigid to subside, so it fell outwards. Evidence for such a collapse was very graphically revealed by excavations south of the East Gate in 1988.[4]

Work on the interpretation of a series of excavations around the Roman circuit has led to the theory that the phase of rebuilding characterised by the reuse of Roman tombstones and architectural fragments coincides with the Aethelfledan refortification.[5] This remains unproven and the evidence is mixed. In some places, the Saxons may well have reused or repaired the masonry wall. Elsewhere, especially where they were extending outwards from the Roman line, they probably built an earthen bank surmounted by a timber palisade. In front of the wall or bank they dug a ditch.

There is some archaeological evidence for Saxon work. During the construction of the Inner Ring Road in 1961-2 on the line of the abandoned western fortress wall, north of the west gate in Linenhall Street, Hugh Thompson excavated a series of large

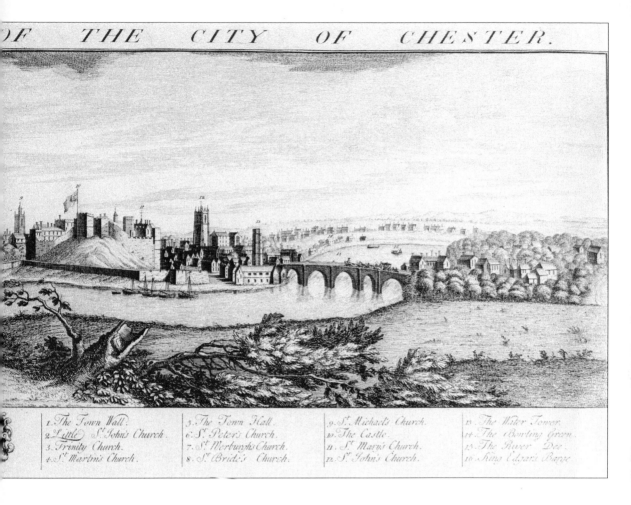

OF THE CITY OF CHESTER.

1. The Town Wall.
2. Little St. John's Church.
3. Trinity Church.
4. St. Martin's Church.
5. The Town Hall.
6. St. Peter's Church.
7. St. Werburgh's Church.
8. St. Bride's Church.
9. St. Michael's Church.
10. The Castle.
11. St. Mary's Church.
12. St. John's Church.
13. The Water Tower.
14. The Bowling Green.
15. The River Dee.
16. King Edgar's Barge

post holes and a beam slot cut into the top of the Roman rampart.[6] He tentatively dated them to the tenth century on account of the presence of Saxon Chester Ware sherds. In addition, the latest ditch on this site lying outside the defences had a U-shaped profile rather than the normal, sharp Roman V-shaped one.[7] This ditch was filled with masonry rubble and, in the absence of other evidence, Thompson interpreted it as Roman.

However, in 1991 another site was excavated across the defensive ditches on the other side of the city, north of the East Gate.[8] This revealed a sequence of Roman and medieval ditches. Cut into the top of the Roman ditches and pre-dating the medieval ones was a masonry rubble-filled ditch similar to the one found at Linenhall Street. This one was more confidently dated for it contained a sherd of Saxon pottery. Since this particular U-shaped ditch was in fact Saxon, it seems likely the western Roman fortress wall was retained in the Saxon circuit, too. It is reasonable to include an extension from the south-eastern corner of the Roman fortress to the river in the Saxon defences because it incorporated the Wolfeld Gate, a place-name with possible Scandinavian associations.[9]

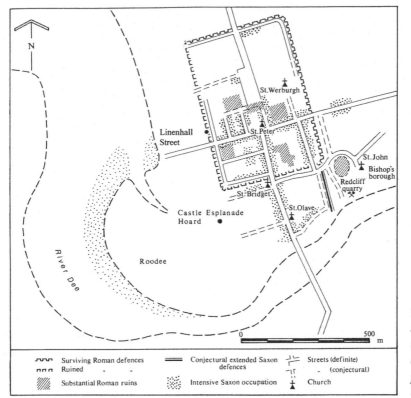

33 *Plan of Saxon Chester in the 10th and 11th centuries, showing possible line of burh defences.*

A topographical feature that may be important to the discussion is a narrow, steep-sided valley, the so-called 'Nuns Field creek', which once ran in a south-westerly direction into the River Dee with its head close to the south-western angle of the fortress walls. At this early period it would have been a substantial obstacle and may even have flooded at high tide. It is possible, therefore, that the Saxon burh defences incorporated the eastern, northern and western Roman walls, with spurs down to the river or the steep valleys from the two southern corners. Only further archaeological discoveries will resolve the mystery.

In 1069-70 the army of William the Conqueror marched across Cheshire from Yorkshire and arrived in Chester. William ordered a castle to be built, a further link in the city's defences, and established a strong earldom with the city as its headquarters. The Norman earldom of Chester was an important and trusted office, one of the marcher lordships that King William founded to protect the border with Wales. Domesday Book reveals that the Earls were the most powerful landowners in the county, the King holding no land in the county himself. William's first appointee, Gherbod the Fleming, did not take up the office, so the line is usually counted from Hugh of Avranches, William's nephew. Avranches in Normandy was not dissimilar to Chester for it lay on the border with Celtic Brittany. The border with Wales was ill-defined and gave the Earls plenty of scope for expansion. They remained powerful throughout the 12th century on account of their land holdings, their loyalty to the Crown and their generally astute political manoeuvring.[10] However, they were unlucky

34 *King William the Conqueror's motte (mound) at Chester Castle, surmounted by the later stone castle.*

in their line of descent. Richard, the 2nd Earl, inherited as a minor and was drowned, heirless, in the White Ship disaster of 1120. He was followed by a cousin, Ranulf I, and then his son, Ranulf II, who successfully negotiated the dangers of the Anarchy in the time of Stephen and Matilda. Ranulf II's son Hugh II was another minor when he inherited in 1153. In spite of rebelling against King Henry II and being imprisoned in Normandy, Hugh retained the earldom of Chester and passed it on to his son, Ranulf III Blundeville, when he died at a young age in 1181.

Ranulf III was the greatest of the Norman earls and held the earldom until his death in 1232. He was instrumental in securing the accession of the young King Henry III after the death of King John in 1216. After that he went on crusade to the Holy Land and on his return commenced the building of Beeston Castle in Cheshire. When he died he left no direct heir and the earldom passed to his sister's son, John the Scot. When he died in 1237, again heirless, only female descendants of Ranulf were left. The lands outside Cheshire were distributed amongst the heirs but the King retained the county and the earldom. In 1254 he granted this to Prince Edward, the future Edward I, and since that time the title has always been held by the monarch's eldest son.

Chester Castle was built by King William to secure as well as protect the city. It became the headquarters for the earldom. Originally, it was an earth and timber 'motte and bailey' castle, typical of those quickly thrown up in the aftermath of the Conquest. The site chosen was a small knoll at the southern corner of the city which lay outside the old Roman fortress and west of

35 *Chester Castle. The Flag Tower was the original Norman stone tower on the motte.*

the main road down to the river crossing (Lower Bridge Street). The position enabled the castle to overlook the bridge, the harbour area and the estuary downstream, as well as dominate the town.

The castle today is the product of a great number of alterations and restorations including an extensive remodelling during the 18th century. But we can still trace elements of the medieval castle and there are paintings and plans of its ancient appearance. We have only limited information for its early development since records of building and expenditure do not survive from the period of the Norman earls. Only when the earl was a minor, and the earldom was managed by the Crown, do the royal accounts provide us with a glimpse of what happened. William's original motte and bailey castle probably only occupied the area that became the inner bailey. The motte can still be discerned from the north though it has

36 *The Agricola Tower, the original 12th-century gate tower at Chester Castle. The chapel of St Mary de Castro is on the first floor.*

been much remodelled by later reconstruction and landscaping. It was presumably once surmounted by a timber tower. The hall of the earls and their other buildings must have lain within the bailey. During the 12th century the timber towers and palisade were rebuilt in stone and two of the towers survive. The Flag Tower, although now the less impressive of the two and in poor repair, is probably the older and is in origin the keep that stood on the top of the motte.

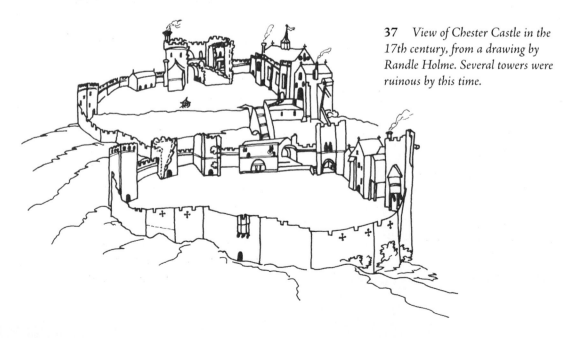

37 *View of Chester Castle in the 17th century, from a drawing by Randle Holme. Several towers were ruinous by this time.*

The other tower is the Agricola Tower, named curiously and misleadingly after a Roman governor of Britain. It has three storeys and was clearly the original gate tower to the castle. The ground floor comprises the blocked gate passage under a stone vault. On the first floor is the castle chapel, St Mary de Castro, a fine, vaulted chamber. It was once elaborately decorated with wall paintings; these were exposed, cleaned and conserved in 1992 but are now (in 2007) sadly almost invisible again.[11] A new gate tower with drum towers flanking the passage was possibly constructed after 1220, when Earl Ranulf III returned from crusade. It lay to the north of the Agricola Tower but no longer survives. Presumably it was at this time that the passage through the Agricola Tower was blocked and it became an ordinary mural tower.

38 *The inner bailey of the castle viewed from the outer bailey. The Great Hall, later the Shire Hall and Exchequer, is on the left.*

At some point a large, new outer bailey was added to the castle and the main accommodation moved out to it. Initially the outer bailey was defended by a bank and palisade, but in 1247-51 this was replaced by stone.[12]

The Norman earls also completed the circuit of the city walls. Wherever the Saxon circuit may have lain, it is clear that the enclosure of the southern and western extensions from the Roman fortress was only completed in the 12th century with a wall built along the river front. Three new gates incorporated into it were the Bridge Gate, the Ship Gate and the Water Gate. The southern side incorporating the Bridge Gate and Ship Gate must have been constructed by the 1120s, for charters of that date record the office of sergeant of those gates, but the western side seems to have been built after the middle of the century.[13]

The city walls when finished comprised the curtain wall itself, gates and towers and a ditch. Most of the towers still survive, though heavily restored over the years. They are only found along the northern and eastern sides. The river was considered sufficient defence along the other two. The towers and gates formed a comprehensive system of flanking cover for the wall face because, unlike the Roman interval towers, they all projected forward. However, they were in a variety of designs, sizes and heights, which suggests that they were built at different times and not to a single overall plan. The simplest are just solid projecting platforms, either rectangular or semi-circular in plan. Morgan's Mount is one such rectangular tower that rises one level above the wall walk with a platform at its top. Others provided more elaborate accommodation. Thimbleby's Tower by the New Gate was semi-octagonal and had a fine, stone-vaulted chamber with cross-bow loops below wall walk level. The Phoenix or King Charles Tower at the north-eastern angle of the Walls has a chamber at wall walk level and another above.

39   *The Phoenix Tower, later known as the King Charles Tower, at the north-eastern corner of the Walls.*

Another well-preserved tower is the Water Tower. Originally known as the New Tower, it was built between 1322 and 1325.[14] It stood in the River Dee and was attached to Bonewaldesthorne's Tower at the north-western angle of the city walls by means of a wide, battlemented spur wall about 30 yards long. The Tower and Spur Wall were built by John de Helpston, who had worked on the king's castles in Wales, and there are great similarities between this tower and a lost Water Tower at Conwy. The contract between de Helpston and the City Corporation is preserved in the city's archives. The tower itself has an upper and lower chamber and was well appointed with a fireplace and garderobe (latrine). Its purpose was to protect the harbour and quays to its south but it also served, no doubt, to monitor shipping movements and ensure that the relevant customs dues were paid. The river silted, however, and by the end of the 16th century the tower had become landlocked; nowadays it lies about 200 yards from the river.

During the Middle Ages there were six major gates and

40   *The Water Tower in the 19th century. When originally built it stood in the river, but by the time of this picture it had long been landlocked.*

41 *The medieval East Gate was flanked by lower towers, also with octagonal corner turrets, which were hidden behind the buildings.*

several posterns. None of the main gates survives *in situ* today as they were all rebuilt in the 18th and 19th centuries to accommodate increased traffic. However, we know something of their appearance from paintings and archaeological discoveries. The East Gate was always the most important entrance to the city. It comprised a tall rectangular tower with octagonal corner turrets and lower flanking towers, also with octagonal turrets. A small part of the northern flanking tower was found in a sewer excavation in 1971.[15] It was built of very fine masonry using cream-coloured sandstone which must have made a striking contrast to the red sandstone commonly used in Chester. We do not know precisely when the East Gate was built but its design appears to have been influenced by Caernarfon Castle, and in 1270 the King acquired land at the East Gate from Agnes de Novo Castello which was confirmed in a writ of 1307.[16] An early 14th-century date therefore seems likely.

The Bridge Gate was strategically important as it guarded the road from North Wales. It opened directly onto the Dee Bridge which was further defended by an outer gate tower at its southern end. The bridge itself was rebuilt in the later 14th century, so the Bridge Gate may also date from that time. The North Gate was a much simpler affair and probably older. The route out of the North Gate was not important and was only used for local access. The gate was a simple rectangular tower with a narrow passageway. Later on it housed the City Gaol, which was noted as a particularly gloomy and unpleasant dungeon.

The other gates, the New Gate, Water Gate and Ship Gate, were simple arched openings. Only the Ship Gate has survived, although not *in situ*; it has been relocated to the Grosvenor Park. The New Gate survives in its 17th-century form and is known by its old name, the Wolf Gate. The modern replacement, now known as the New Gate, was built alongside it in

42 *The medieval North Gate after the canal had been dug.*

the 1938. Of the posterns, the most interesting survivor is the Kaleyard Gate in the eastern wall. In 1275 the monks of St Werburgh's Abbey petitioned Edward I to allow them to cut a gate through the Walls to their vegetable garden which lay just beyond them at this point. Permission was granted with the proviso that they ensured it was locked at nightfall, a duty which endures to this day.

Surrounding the walls on the landward sides was a ditch. The Saxon ditch had been deliberately infilled with rubble and masonry. The medieval ditch lay further out from the wall face, presumably to accommodate the projecting towers and gates. In 1991 a section across the sequence of three medieval ditches was excavated near the East Gate.[17] The earliest ditch was wide but shallow, only a little over a metre in depth, and perhaps unfinished. The Chronicle of St Werburgh's Abbey provides a possible reason.[18] In 1264, during the Barons' War, the citizens feared attack by the Barons or the Welsh and William la Zouche, the justiciary, and Robert Mercer, the Sheriff, commenced digging a ditch round the city. However, following the Battle of Lewes in 1264 and the capture of King Henry III and his son Edward, Chester was granted to Simon de Montfort who installed his own justiciary, Lucas de Taney. The next year, 1265, Prince Edward led a resurgence of the King's party and his men besieged Lucas de Taney in Chester Castle for ten weeks. Simon de Montfort was killed at the Battle of Evesham and Lucas submitted to Edward. These events might explain why the first ditch was abandoned.

The second ditch was much more substantial, being 7½ feet deep, and may well have been associated with the construction of the new East Gate in the early 14th century. Each ditch became filled in time with a valuable deposit of archaeological remains because the inhabitants used them for rubbish disposal. These deposits remained waterlogged and were rich in organic materials – wood, leather, plants and insects – that do not usually survive well in Chester, as well as the more common finds of pottery and bones. They show that leather workers and cobblers were working in the vicinity, disposing of their scraps and worn-out shoes in the ditch.

43 *The arch of the Ship Gate, now relocated to the Grosvenor Park.*

The end of the 13th century marked a high point in military activity in Chester and also in the city's prosperity. The border with Wales had been persistently turbulent since the Norman Conquest and King Edward I resolved on settling it once and for all. When the Welsh Prince Llewellyn failed to pay fealty and make his annual payments, Edward decided on a campaign of conquest. Chester became his main base. Military campaigns were fought in 1277 and, again, in 1282-3 and 1294-5 following renewed Welsh revolts. These campaigns differed from earlier ones, however, by the construction of the series of massive castles that still dominate the North Wales coastline. They enabled Edward to retain control of the conquered areas beyond the immediate campaigning season. The building of the castles involved a major effort and huge resources. Men, materials and supplies were conscripted from across England and Ireland and

44 *The Wolf Gate in its 17th-century form. Before the New Gate was built, in 1938, this was one of the main entries into the city.*

passed through Chester on their way into North Wales.[19] Many workmen would have stayed in the city over winter when building work was suspended. The building programme began in 1277 and continued unbroken until the end of the century. Work was still being carried on sporadically at Caernarfon and Beaumaris Castles until the 1320s, though neither was ever completed. From 1298 Edward I and his son Edward II became embroiled in wars in Scotland and attention and resources were diverted there.

It is not surprising therefore to find that this was a particularly prosperous period for the citizens of Chester and that it resulted in fine new buildings like the Water Tower and, probably, the East Gate. More building work was also undertaken at Chester Castle, including chambers for the King and Queen and a new outer gatehouse (1292-3).[20]

One noteworthy individual connected with these activities was Master Richard Lenginour (the Engineer). He worked at Caernarfon and Beaumaris Castles under Master James of St George, the Master of the King's Works.[21] But Edward I also granted him in 1275 a daily wage of 12d. for work at Chester and the farm of the Dee Mills (but he had to grind King's corn for free in time of war). Richard had a stone mansion in Lower Bridge Street which extended from St Olave's church to Claverton Lane (Duke Street),[22] and has been identified as the architect who completed the rebuilding of the choir of St Werburgh's Abbey. He received payments from the Abbot

45 *A section across the city ditches, excavated in 1991. They had been filled with refuse.*

in 1310 and 1312-13 for the work.[23] Richard served as Mayor of Chester in 1305-06 and became a country gentleman, acquiring land in Eccleston, Eaton and Poulton, south of the city. His moated manor site at Belgrave in Eccleston seems to have been an early example of a formal, designed garden.[24] He died in 1315 and his Lower Bridge Street house passed to his son Almaricus, who sold it five years later.

For most of the later medieval period, Chester was less embroiled in military activity and a final recutting of the city ditch was probably devised mainly to assist drainage through what had become a noisome trench filled with rotting rubbish. However, many Cheshire men served with King Edward III and the Black Prince, who also held the earldom of Chester, in the wars in France. Throughout the 14th century, sums of money were spent on the castle, to maintain both the accommodation and the defences. At the end of the century, Chester and Cheshire men suffered for their support of Richard II.[25] In 1399 Henry Duke of Lancaster occupied Chester Castle and seized King Richard, who was at Flint. Richard, deserted by his followers, was brought to Henry at Chester and subsequently forced to abdicate and the Duke was proclaimed King Henry IV. Sir Peter Legh of Lyme was executed and had his head stuck on a pike over the East Gate. There were pro-Yorkist disturbances in 1400 and Sir Peter's head was rescued and buried with his body at the White Friary. After the Battle of Shrewsbury in 1403, a quarter of the body of Henry Percy (Hotspur) was sent to Chester to be hung from the gates, together with the heads of Sir Richard Venables and Richard de Vernon, a grim warning to would-be rebels against the Lancastrian regime.

Chapter 5

The Medieval City – Trade and Clerics

At the time of the Norman Conquest Chester was a wealthy and relatively populous place. Population statistics for this time are inevitably vague but a recent estimate puts it at 2,500-3,000.[1] Domesday Book records that in 1066 the city was worth £45. It also records a complex system of fines and customs that indicates a well-organised and active port. Trade with Ireland was well developed, the import of pelts being noted. The return trade may well have included salt. There were 487 houses. But by 1071, when Earl Hugh received it, the city was worth only £30, there were 282 houses and it was described as greatly waste. By 1086 the farm of the city had increased to £70 and there is growing archaeological evidence to show that there was wholesale reorganisation of property and landholdings within the city at this period. It resulted in the typical medieval pattern of long strips or burgage plots and concentration of buildings on the street frontages with much open space behind them.[2]

As well as building the castle and completing the city walls, the Normans introduced several important new institutions into the city. In 1075 Peter, Bishop of Lichfield, moved the seat of his see to Chester. The church of St John the Baptist, just outside the city walls and reputed to be the oldest church in the city, became his cathedral. The Bishop, canons and ecclesiastical officers had residences around the church and the area was known as the Bishop's Borough. Peter died in 1085. A remarkable memento of him was discovered in the 1960s in a late medieval pit excavated on the Old Market Hall site, the lead seal matrix with which he would have sealed documents. It should have been broken on his death but the story of how it came to be dropped in a pit hundreds of years later is now lost in the mists of time. St John's status as a cathedral did not endure and by 1102 Peter's successor, Robert de Limesey, had moved to Coventry. The bishops maintained their connection with the city and early in the 12th century St John's embarked on an ambitious rebuilding programme, work continuing throughout the century. It was probably intended to have two western towers but only one was ever built. It dominated the Chester skyline until it collapsed in 1881. Half of this fine Romanesque church survives in use; the rest is ruined.

47 *The lead seal matrix of Bishop Peter (1075-85) with its impression below.*

46 *The church of St John the Baptist as it appeared in the 19th century. It was originally much longer, the ruins of the east end lying in the trees on the left.*

In 1093 Earl Hugh converted the other major church, St Werburgh's, into a Benedictine abbey. A party of monks from the abbey of Bec in Normandy came to Chester to form the nucleus of the new monastery, Richard of Bec being their first abbot. What is believed to be his stone coffin was found under the cloister of the abbey in 1997. Unfortunately, it had been disturbed in the past and was empty, but it could have accommodated a person well over six feet tall. Earl Hugh endowed his new abbey generously and encouraged his retainers to do likewise and it became one of the richest abbeys in the country. The abbey precinct occupied all the north-eastern quarter of the city within the walls. At first the monks used the existing Saxon church, but they immediately started building their abbey church to its east. Parts of the Norman abbey church and cloisters survive in the present cathedral. Earl Hugh died in 1101 and was buried in the abbey. In 1120 his body was translated to the newly completed chapter house, as befitted his status as founder.

48 *The magnificent 12th-century interior of St John the Baptist.*

49 *The ruins of the eastern end of St John's church, with the Norman chancel arch on the left. The eastern arm of the church was demolished in the 16th century, after the Dissolution, because it was too big for its parishioners.*

During the Norman period Chester also received its full complement of parish churches: St Mary's, St Michael's, Holy Trinity and St Martin's were all founded around this time.

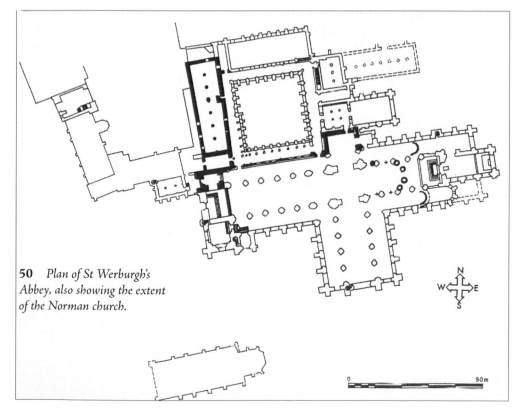

50 *Plan of St Werburgh's Abbey, also showing the extent of the Norman church.*

51   *The chancel arch from the nunnery, relocated to Grosvenor Park.*

Earl Ranulf II founded a Benedictine nunnery around 1150 on a site just north of the castle. It was always small and poor compared with the abbey but it seems to have enjoyed the affection of the citizens. The prioress was often a member of a local family. No physical remains of the nunnery have survived *in situ* above ground but the chancel arch of the church does survive. It stands in the Grosvenor Park, to where it was moved in the 19th century.

The earls are also credited with the construction of the Dee Mills at the city end of the Dee Bridge. The mills were fed by a head of water created by building a causeway or weir upstream from the bridge. They held a monopoly over all milling in Chester and so became immensely profitable. Only the abbot, the nunnery and a few chosen individuals were exempt from the monopoly, which the earls leased out to various operators. The wealth of the millers of the Dee was legendary and many were prominent citizens. But the monopoly was evidently a bone of contention with the citizens. In 1237, at the death of Earl John, there was a riot in which the mills were torn down. The King restored them and they returned to profitability. One of the later lessees was Richard Lenginour and he carried out much building work and improvement following flood damage.

The earls of Chester established the castle as their base and entertained the King there during royal

52   *The High Cross, removed after the Civil War siege, was restored to its old position in 1977.*

expeditions against either the Welsh or Irish, including Henry II in 1157 and 1165 and John in 1211. They were important figures nationally, with extensive estates elsewhere in England and abroad, and so were frequently absent from Chester. Inevitably a bureaucracy developed to run the city for them. There was a justice and two chamberlains and the constable of the castle and the clerk, as well as the earl's reeve and the sheriff of Chester. In the early years of the Norman earldom the city was kept under close control and the revenues collected by their officers were an important source of the earls' income.

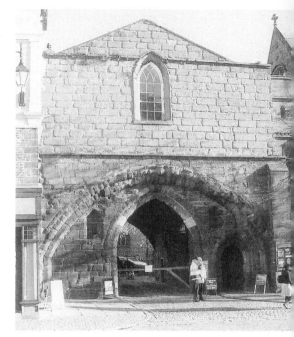

In time, however, the citizens gained more independence to manage their own affairs. The sheriff remained the earl's principal officer and presided over the portmote court, which dealt with property issues and was held in the Common Hall or Moot Hall on Commonhall Lane behind Bridge Street. The burgesses held their property in the city by payment of a gable

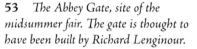

53 *The Abbey Gate, site of the midsummer fair. The gate is thought to have been built by Richard Lenginour.*

rent to the earl, rather than by service. Charters confirmed their rights to hold their customary fairs and markets and to pursue their trade in Dublin. The main market place was at the Cross, where the four main streets of Chester met in front of St Peter's church. The other was in the wide part of Northgate Street, outside the Abbey Gate. The abbey had the privilege of holding the main annual fair outside its gate during midsummer, at the time of which trading elsewhere in the city was prohibited. A second fair was held at Michaelmas. Lucian, a monk of St Werburgh's, wrote a description of Chester 'De Laude Cestrie' in about 1195.[3] He was much taken with the Christian symbolism of the four streets meeting at the Cross and the various parish churches. He notes the importance of the fish in the Dee and merchant ships from Aquitaine, Ireland, Spain and Germany. He describes the citizens as cheerful and hospitable, impatient of control and not knowing the meaning of hard work!

The 13th century saw the emergence of the major city offices. By the 1230s there were two sheriffs. At about the same time the city became responsible for the farm – an annual payment due to the earl. Shortly after, around 1240, there is the first mention of a mayor, William the Clerk. This office soon became the senior post and the mayor was recognised as the chief representative of the citizens. He presided over the pentice court which, amongst other matters, regulated trade and was held in the Pentice, a 'lean-to' structure built against the south and east sides of St Peter's church. In such a location, the mayor was well placed to keep an eye on the market and the pillory. In spite of its name and restricted site, the Pentice must have been quite a grand structure. On the ground floor were shops and above were chambers known as the inner and outer pentice. Civic banquets were held in these rooms in which important guests, including on occasion the King, were entertained. A charter obtained from Edward I in 1300 confirmed the offices and the city's rights and set the farm at £100 a year. A major concession was the granting to the mayor and sheriffs of the right to hear the pleas of the crown.

By this period, too, the leading traders had formed a guild merchant. Ireland remained the major trading partner, with the import of foodstuffs, especially corn and also hides, being notable. The wine trade with Gascony was also important and fine pottery was imported from the wine-producing areas. The merchants who participated in this trade became important figures, often filling the civic offices. Particularly noteworthy was the family of William of Doncaster, several members bearing this name. William of Doncaster II had a large mansion with shops and undercrofts in Watergate Street in the late 13th century as well as property throughout the city. William III prospered in royal service, victualling the armies and garrisons in North Wales during Edward I's campaigns. He acquired land and offices in Wirral and North Wales and served as mayor in 1301, 1315-16 and 1317-19, although his fortunes declined after the death of Edward II. He was followed by William IV and V, the latter being sheriff in 1343-4, the last of the Doncasters to hold civic office.

As the major regional centre and market, Chester had the usual complement of food and service trades, such as butchers, bakers, vintners and brewers, some

54 *The Rows of Chester, which line the four main streets of the city, are galleries which run through the first floors of the buildings and have been in existence at least since the 13th century.*

55 *A view along Rows in Watergate Street. The medieval building on the left may have been the house of William of Doncaster. Medieval stone arches span the Row in the distance.*

of whose businesses were concentrated in specific areas of the city. A speciality of Chester was the leather industry, although not all the leather trades enjoyed the same status. Glovers and saddlers had premises in Bridge Street in the centre of the city. Skinners were prominent in civic life in the early 13th century. There were also cobblers and shoemakers, tanners and tawyers. The tanners were at the bottom of the scale. Because of their size and the obnoxious odours they emitted, the tanneries were situated outside the Walls in places such as St John Street. As the suburbs expanded, they were displaced further and further along Foregate Street. Tanning pits are known from excavations in this area.

56 *A fine vaulted and aisled undercroft in Watergate Street at street level. They are known colloquially but incorrectly as crypts. The hall would originally have occupied the floor above.*

57 *A vaulted undercroft at 12 Bridge Street. Unusually, this example has a wall staircase, making it accessible from the floor above. It had been infilled with earth and refuse, but was rediscovered and emptied out in 1839.*

The wealthy citizens lived in some style. Many medieval houses survive in Chester often hidden behind more recent frontages. Rows, the galleries that run through the fronts of the houses at first-floor level, are found on the four main streets. They are unique to Chester. The Rows gave access to the main living accommodation, the first-floor halls, most of which lay at right angles to the street and had a central fireplace. As the long sides formed party walls with their neighbours, these halls were dark places, any smoke finding its way out through louvres in the roof. At the row front there may have been separate shops, but in the smaller examples the hall itself doubled as the shop.[4] A chamber above the Row, the 'solar', provided more private accommodation. In larger examples the hall lay parallel to the street and may have had several shops

58 *Medieval cess and rubbish pits, in the back yards of the house on Lower Bridge Street, excavated in 1974.*

59 *Reconstruction painting of a medieval back yard in Watergate Street, with kitchens, pig sties, privies and rubbish pits.*

along the row frontage. At street level were undercrofts which were frequently stone-built, the better examples having fine ribbed vaults. These provided excellent premises for safely storing and selling valuable goods. Many were built during the prosperous times of the 13th century. More accommodation lay at the rear of the hall along with service rooms. The kitchen could have been a free-standing building in the long yard which lay behind the house. Sanitation was primitive and the back yards were used for cess pits and rubbish disposal. With such closely packed buildings, fire was an ever-present danger and serious fires occurred in 1140, 1180 and 1278. In 1180 the fire was reputedly brought under control only when the monks paraded the relics of St Werburgh through the streets.[5] On 15 May 1278, fire is said to have burned almost the whole of Chester within the walls.[6]

Domestic water supply in the city appears to have been very inadequate. There were few wells for private use and drawers brought water from the Dee around the city.

In the 13th century the landscape of the city was further transformed by the arrival of the friars. Unlike the monks, who established communities isolated from the world, the friars were set up to work in the community, teaching, preaching and administering to the poor. They became very popular and had powerful friends. Three orders of friars established houses in Chester. First to arrive, in about 1236 and under the patronage of Alexander de Stavensby, Bishop of Lichfield, were the Dominicans, also known as Friars Preachers or Black Friars. The Earl granted them a large block of land on the western side of the city between the nunnery and Watergate Street.[7] Although close to the harbour and within the city walls, there was still much open land in this area and it was known as the Crofts. There was an old chapel to St Nicholas on the site which the friars took over.

The Franciscans or Grey Friars followed, in 1237-8, and were granted land to the north of Watergate Street. The Dominicans and de Stavensby opposed the new foundation because they feared there would be insufficient alms to support two friaries so close together. But they were persuaded in a letter from Bishop Robert Grosseteste

of Lincoln that the alms would actually grow to meet whatever were the needs, like a living fountain of water increasing as it is drawn.[8]

The third order to establish a permanent home in Chester was the Carmelites or White Friars. The community is recorded in 1277 but did not acquire its own house until 1290 when Hugh Payn granted it seven messuages in the suburbs. Hugh owned land near the Bars in Foregate Street and the first house may have been there.[9] However, during the 1290s the friars were established in their permanent home to the west of Bridge Street in the lane still called White Friars.

The friaries became well-established and popular. Many citizens wished to be buried in their churches or graveyards, and funerals and the subsequent services, memorial masses and chantries were an important source of income to churches, so the rights were jealously guarded. In Chester, only St John's and

60 *The fine tombstone for Agnes of Ridley (d. 1347) in St John's church.*

61 *Burials in the Black Friary church, excavated in 1977.*

St Werburgh's churches had anciently possessed such burial rights, but the friars came to an agreement whereby they could carry out funerals, too. However, the proceeds from funerals of citizens and people who by ancient custom should have been buried in St Werburgh's or St John's had to be divided between the three churches. The friars were allowed to keep all the proceeds from the burial of strangers.[10]

As the friaries prospered, they built themselves fine churches and cloisters. These important features in the townscape of medieval Chester have now totally disappeared but we know something of their appearance from archaeology. The Black Friary has been most thoroughly

62   *Reconstruction of the Black Friary, based on excavated evidence.*

investigated.[11] The early, simple, chapel was expanded during the 13th century by the addition of a wide, aisled, preaching nave. The friars built a pipeline in 1276 from springs in Boughton, a mile away, to bring water to their house. They were granted permission to open and close the land and to pierce the city wall with the pipes. They hosted the provincial chapter of their order in 1312. Later in the century the friars rebuilt their church with graceful octagonal piers and decorated tile floors. Decorated floors and elaborate grave slabs have been found at the Grey Friary, too.[12]

   The abbey was a hive of building activity during the Middle Ages. In the mid-13th century, the monks rebuilt their living quarters and chapter house and improved their water supply. Firstly, in 1278, a conduit was led from a spring in Newton Fields north of the city, and then in 1282 they were granted a spring in Christleton, three miles to the east, at a site still known as Abbot's Well. They built a pipeline from there to the cistern in the cloister. The surplus water flushed the latrine attached to the dormitory. This had a fine masonry drain, tall enough to stand up in, which still survives in remarkably good condition under the Cathedral Green. From about 1260, the monks set out on an ambitious programme to rebuild their church. It would take them 260 years. At the east end, outside the existing church, Abbot Simon de Whitchurch commenced with the Lady Chapel and choir. Simon died in 1291 and

63   *Part of the bone frame from a pair of spectacles excavated on the Black Friary site. The friars had an important library and some of the books are now in Shrewsbury School.*

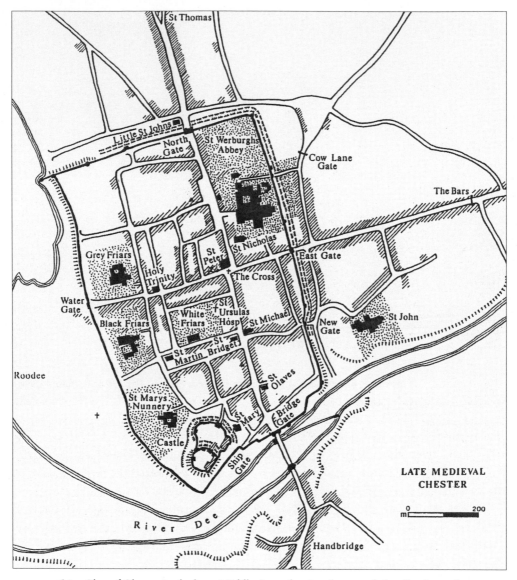

64   *Plan of Chester in the later Middle Ages, showing the extended walls, the castle
and the extensive religious precincts.*

was replaced by Thomas de Burchelles who continued the building work at a difficult time because masons were in high demand and sometimes conscripted for the King's works in Wales. The choir was finished by Master Richard Lenginour after 1310. The work was carried on throughout the 14th century, first with the crossing tower and then the south transept and the nave.

The abbey at this time was home to the monk Ranulf Higden, who entered the monastery in 1299 and whilst there wrote several books. Most important was the *Polychronicon*, a widely read history book starting with the biblical creation and continuing until Ranulf's own time. Such was his reputation that in 1352 he was

65 *A 17th-century engraving of the abbey by Daniel King.*

summoned to Westminster to advise King Edward III's council. He died in 1364 and was buried in the south choir aisle of the abbey church.

There were two hospitals in medieval Chester to care for the sick and infirm. Little St John's outside the North Gate was established by Earl Ranulf III in 1190. St Giles at Boughton, about a mile east of Chester, was the leper hospital. It lay on the main road so that the inmates could beg travellers for alms. A third, added in 1510, was dedicated to St Ursula and founded by a bequest of Roger Smith. It lay in Commonhall Lane and the Common Hall, by then disused, served as its chapel.

In 1349 the Black Death swept through the city. Only a few records of its devastating effects have been preserved. Abbot William Bebington died in that year and so did the prioress of the nunnery. The rents of the Dee Mills were reduced by a third and still struggled to make a profit,[13] and for the next century the city was much less prosperous, empty shops and neglected buildings being recorded.[14] A decline in civil and religious life can also be discerned and Abbot Richard Sainsbury (1349-62) was forced to resign due to bad governance. The friars

66 *The 13th-century abbey latrine, recently rediscovered and still functioning.*

were not infrequently mentioned in the city's records for their involvement in riotous and violent fracas, though the Franciscans were notable by their absence from these events.[15] Edward, the Black Prince and Earl of Chester, always eager to maximise his income from the earldom, considered the city full of evil doers. In 1349 Mayor Bartholomew of Northendon was murdered by a former sheriff.

One necessary project that was undertaken was the replacement of the Old Dee Bridge. There had been a crossing at the time of the Norman Conquest which may well have been the original Roman bridge. It was apparently built of stone piers with a timber carriageway, a typical Roman form. Periodic repairs were recorded through the next two centuries but in 1279/80 the timber part was swept away. The 14th century was a period of climatic deterioration, rising sea levels and increasingly stormy weather.[16] Bridge repair work is recorded in the 1340s, 1350s and most significantly in 1387, when the citizens were allowed to divert the murage (a toll raised for repairing the walls) to it. The work undoubtedly resulted in the stone bridge that survives to this day. By then, too, the silting of the Dee was becoming a problem. Ships found it difficult to reach the quays at Chester and goods were frequently unloaded into lighters downstream. In 1445 the annual farm paid by the city to the King was reduced from £100 to £50 and in 1484 to £30.

At the end of the 14th century the abbey was beautified under the patronage of King Richard II. The fine carved choir stalls dating from about 1390 are believed to be the work of William and Hugh Herland, the King's master carpenters, who were also responsible for the stalls at Lincoln Cathedral. The numerous decorated floor tiles which have been found in the nave are of this period also. It would appear, therefore, that even though the church was still unfinished, perhaps with a temporary roof, it was furnished and used.

67 *The Old Dee Bridge, built in the 14th century.*

68 *View of Chester from the south-west. The quays outside the Ship Gate and below the castle can be seen downstream of the bridge with the Dee Mills at its city end. The church of St John's rises in the background. The tall tower by the mills is the 17th-century Tyrer's Water Tower.*

In the later 15th century the fortunes of the city revived and records become more plentiful. From this time dates the emergence of craft guilds in addition to the merchant guild. Most of the trades in the city developed their own guild in order to regulate their trade, control prices, establish conditions for apprenticeships and provide social services such as funerals for their members. They tried to establish monopolies for themselves, banning strangers and non-members from trading. However, the castle demesne and the abbey precincts were outside the city's liberties and non-guild members could trade there. Leather workers, in particular, congregated by the castle in the area which became known as the Gloverstone. The lane which ran along the riverbank below the castle became known as Skinners Lane. Strictures against the Welsh were even more harsh. An enduring tradition claims that Welsh men were banished from the city after dark and could be legally shot with a crossbow.

The other major activity of the guilds was to put on the cycle of mystery plays. These developed into one of the great festivals of the city in the 15th century. They were held initially as part of the Corpus Christi procession but were moved to Whitsun before 1521. The cycle, which

69 *A 14th-century floor tile from the abbey. The design is ultimately derived from wall paintings in ninth-century Buddhist caves in western China and presumably reached Chester via the Silk Road.*

70 *The Old Leche House in Watergate Street. Rebuilt in the late Middle Ages and again in the 17th century, it retains its medieval open hall.*

has survived in copies, tells the story of the Bible from the Creation to the Last Judgement in 24 plays. Each guild or group of guilds was responsible for a particular play. Some were particularly appropriate: the Drawers of Dee put on Noah and the Flood, the Carpenters the Nativity, and the Bakers the Last Supper. The plays were performed on carts that were moved around the city in sequence, starting at the Abbey Gate and visiting the Cross and the four main streets. The guilds vied with each other to put on the most spectacular and elaborate show.

Evidence of an ecclesiastical revival at the end of the 15th century can be seen in a series of major building projects. At St Werburgh's Abbey, Abbot Simon Ripley (1485-93) put the finances in order and recommended the building work which would lead at long last to the completion of the abbey church and then the rebuilding of the cloisters. The White Friary church was rebuilt with a tall tower and steeple in 1495. The Grey Friars also had their church rebuilt, but a charter of 1528 records their agreement to permit the merchants and sailors of Chester to use the nave and aisles of the church, which the merchants and sailors had built, for storing sails and equipment.[17] Clearly the Grey Friars no longer had the personnel or resources to rebuild and use their church. Excavation at the Black Friary showed that rebuilding was planned there, too, but had not progressed beyond the foundations when the Dissolution came.[18]

Renewed building works did not extend to secular society at this time,[19] although the Old Leche House in Watergate Street is an important exception. It was rebuilt on an older undercroft and incorporated the innovation of a fireplace with chimneybreast, though still containing an open hall. The Middle Ages ended with the dramatic events of the Dissolution which, in Chester at least, passed off quietly. On 15 August 1538 the King's commissioner, Richard Ingworth, received the surrender of all three friaries. The abbey followed on 20 January 1540 and, the next day, the nunnery. The sites and lands of these institutions, perhaps a fifth of the area of the city, suddenly passed into private ownership.

Chapter 6

County Town and Civil Strife – the Sixteenth and Seventeenth Centuries

T he century which followed the end of the Middle Ages was bracketed by two cataclysmic events, the dissolution of the religious houses by Henry VIII and the Civil War between King Charles I and Parliament. Both had a dramatic effect on Chester. Although, from our distant perspective, the intervening period appears peaceful and uneventful, important changes unfolded. Between 1538 and 1541 large areas of land formerly enclosed in religious precincts passed into lay ownership. The population had recovered to its pre-Black Death levels and continued to grow. New fashions, styles and expectations were making themselves felt and the period was one of expansion and redevelopment. At the same time, Chester's significance on the national stage declined although it remained an important regional centre. The river and harbour continued to silt. The opening of the New World, which so benefited Bristol at this time and would later furnish prosperity to Liverpool, largely passed Chester by. The city was still an important port for the crossing to Ireland but increasingly embarkation occurred at out-ports further down the river. The Merchant Adventurers Company founded in 1553 constructed Newquay, and when the Earl of Leicester's expedition to Ireland passed through Chester in 1583 it embarked from there. But Newquay proved to be only a temporary solution for it soon became silted too.[1]

The city remained quietly prosperous and rebuilding and refurbishment of the housing stock carried on. Most people still lived on the main streets, where the houses incorporating the Rows provided space for their craft, manufacturing or retail activities. Timber framing, which gives Chester its characteristic 'black and white' appearance, was still the most common building technique. However, new styles were appearing and fireplaces with chimneys replaced central open hearths. Sometimes they were constructed of brick. The open halls which had been the heart of the medieval house were replaced by more private chambers on upper floors. Bishop Lloyds Palace (1615) in Watergate Street has fine panelled rooms with decorated plaster ceilings and chimneypieces in the main chambers above the Row.[2] In the medieval period, these would have been the solar and the main room would have been the hall at Row level.

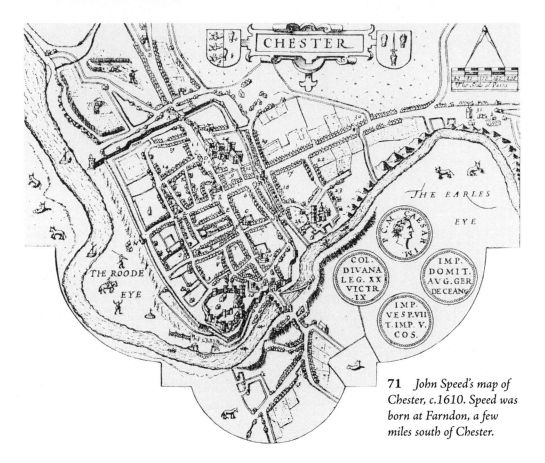

71 *John Speed's map of Chester, c.1610. Speed was born at Farndon, a few miles south of Chester.*

The precincts of the dissolved religious houses provided an opportunity for more expansive development away from the cramped medieval street frontages. Stanley Palace, built in 1597 on the Black Friary site, was approached via a courtyard opening off the street. The hall behind the front door was a low, relatively small room. Again, the main chamber was on the upper floor. Another building on the Black Friary site was later excavated at Nicholas Street Mews. It contained a brick fireplace and garderobe pit and other evidence for improved standards of living such as a much greater range and quantity of pottery. Clay pipes appear and are evidence of the introduction of tobacco, one of the commodities imported from the New World. Tobacco pipe production was established in Chester at an early date and developed into an important if small-scale industry.[3]

Increased population led to development on the minor streets. The suburbs grew along the roads out of the city, especially on Foregate Street to the east and Handbridge south of the river. But much open land still remained within the walled area.

One potentially severe effect of the Dissolution was mitigated by the refoundation of St Werburgh's Abbey as the cathedral for a new diocese of Chester, one of six created nationally by Henry VIII, and so the abbey church and buildings survived. The event was not particularly distressing for the personnel either. The

72 *Timber-framed buildings in Watergate Street; many dating from the 16th and 17th centuries. The richly decorated building on the right is Bishop Lloyd's House.*

73 *An ornate chimney breast and plaster ceiling in Bishop Lloyd's House.*

last abbot became the first Dean of the new Chapter, and several of the monks became canons. Sub-Dean William Wall was previously Warden of the Grey Friary. However, this could be a disturbing time for those following a clerical profession. The Protestant principles espoused under Edward VI were reversed following a return to Catholicism under Mary and reversed again under the settlement of Elizabeth. Sub-Dean Wall survived all the changes and was buried in the cathedral in 1573 under the west window, but others were not so accommodating. George Marsh espoused Protestant beliefs and refused to recant under Mary. In 1555 he was tried at the Consistory Court in the cathedral and was found guilty of heresy. His judges were

74   *Carving from the frontage of Bishop Lloyd's House showing biblical scenes: Adam and Eve, Cain and Abel, and Abraham and Isaac.*

those who had trimmed their beliefs to the changing winds and he did not fail to point out the embarrassment of their position.[4] But this did not save him from being burned at the stake at Boughton where a monument to him now stands.

The foundation of the cathedral included the King's School for 24 'poor and friendless' boys under a master and usher.[5] The scholars were housed in various, generally unsuitable, parts of the old abbey buildings where they were in danger of injury from falling stones. At different times they occupied buildings in the abbey court, St Nicholas chapel and even the south transept. By the early 17th century they had settled in the old refectory where their graffiti may still be seen carved into the sandstone walls.

Although the smaller religious houses had all been dissolved, their buildings were not immediately demolished. The nunnery next to the castle was bought by the Brereton family. A contemporary plan shows that they converted the outer court and probably the prioress' house into their town house whilst the church and cloister fell into ruin. The White

75   *Stanley Palace, Watergate Street, built in 1591 on the former precinct of the dissolved Black Friary.*

76 *The Bishop's Throne in the cathedral as rebuilt in 1635, using the shrine of St Werburgh as its base. (C.J. Hullmandel after John Skinner Prout)*

Friary precinct was divided between two major land holders but the ruined nave of the church with its graceful spire survived. Its eventual destruction in 1597 was much lamented by local, 17th-century antiquarian Randle Holme (the third of that name), who showed surprisingly modern concerns:

> The curious spier steeple might still have stood grace to the citty had not privat benefite the devourer of antiquitie pulled it downe wth the church and erected a house for man's comodity wch since hath been of little use that the Citie lost so goodly an ornament that tymes hereafter may more talk of it …[6]

The house in question was built for Thomas Egerton, the Queen's Attorney General.

The peace of the city was interrupted by the outbreak of the English Civil War in 1642. Chester was more heavily involved in the war, and for a longer period, than many places. Active military campaigning generally swept over towns, so they were involved in fighting for only a short period, but Chester remained on the front line throughout the conflict.

The immediate cause of the breach between King and Parliament was the command of the army raised to put down a Catholic rebellion which flared up in Ireland in the autumn of 1641. Chester became involved insofar as it was still the main port for Ireland and many local gentry families had estates in that country. During 1642 soldiers and equipment gathered at the city to be sent across the Irish Sea. The city also hosted Protestant refugees from the fighting. One of the MPs for Cheshire was Sir William Brereton, an ardent Protestant and critic of the King. On 8 August he came to the city with supporters, beating a drum at the Cross and trying to raise troops, but was surrounded by a hostile crowd, arrested by the mayor and ejected. King Charles was also raising troops and by the autumn was in Shrewsbury. From there, between 23 and 28 September 1642, he visited Chester and was welcomed as was customary by the mayor and corporation and entertained in the Pentice.

Chester was by inclination and tradition royalist, and the arrival of the King and his soldiers served to place the city firmly in the royalist fold. Parliamentarians in the city were either arrested or fled. However, after the King left many local Royalists marched with him, potential defenders who would be missed in the years to come. Little action was anticipated in Cheshire and it was assumed that the conflict would be settled quickly elsewhere. The gates and drawbridges were repaired and a regular watch was maintained, but otherwise little was done. However, the campaign of 1642 between the two main armies was inconclusive so King and Parliament looked to their supporters across the country and prepared for a longer war. Chester was important to the royalist cause because of its connections with Ireland, where there was a strong force

77 *Monument to George Marsh in Boughton, close to where he was burnt at the stake for heresy in 1555.*

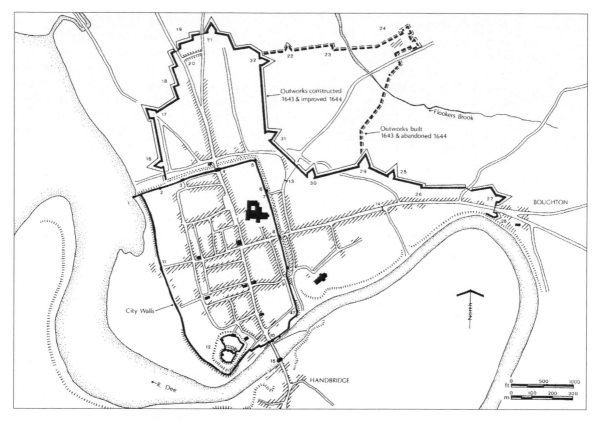

78   *Plan of the outworks as originally built in 1643 and modified in 1644.*

loyal to the King, and with North Wales, an important royalist recruiting ground.
Colonel Ellis, a professional soldier, was sent by the King to supervise the construction
of modern defence works around the city. The technology of warfare had moved on
since the city walls were constructed and tall masonry walls were not thought adequate
to withstand cannon fire. Moreover, the city had considerably outgrown the walls on
the north and east and many wealthy citizens had houses in the suburbs. So these were
defended by a line of earthworks, the so-called 'mud walls', earth and timber ramparts
and ditches being easy to build and better able to absorb cannon fire. The line ran from
the North Wall, across Further North Gate Street, out to Hoole Lane and Flookers
Brook and down to the River Dee at Boughton.[7] Nothing of this line survives above
ground and we only know of its course and appearance from contemporary descriptions
and a map drawn by William Cowper in the 1760s. Although Cowper was working
more than a century after the event, he was a direct descendant of Thomas Cowper,
the mayor in 1642, so he may well have had access to original information.[8]

    This line was over-ambitious. It may reflect an intended role for Chester as base
and staging-post for troops brought across from Ireland. But it seems unlikely that
the line could have been completed to a satisfactory strength and it would have been
too long for just the garrison of the local trained band and Welsh regiments to man
effectively. It was not seriously tested during 1643. Sir William Brereton MP was

79 *Thomas Cowper, mayor in 1641-2, demonstrates his Royalist credentials by the pendant which depicts a bust of Charles I.*

appointed commander of the Parliamentary forces in Cheshire and he returned to the county in January. Chester was denied to him so he took Nantwich and made that town his headquarters for the duration of the war. Although the west of the county, including Chester, was mainly royalist, the east had Parliamentary sympathies. During early 1643 Brereton established his position in eastern Cheshire by capturing Warrington and Stafford, thereby securing his communications with Lancashire and the Parliamentary heartlands in London and the South East.

Chester suffered its first casualties of the war in July when Parliamentary raids on the outworks were beaten off.[9] By November Brereton was ready to move against the city, his strategy being to blockade it by cutting off its supply line to Wales. His troops seized the bridge at Holt, upstream from Chester, on 8 November and marched round to cut the coast road at Hawarden, but in the nick of time 3,000 troops from the King's army in Ireland landed at Mostyn and marched into Chester. They were joined by a force of cavalry from Oxford under John, Lord Byron, who assumed the governorship of the city. Brereton's troops were forced to withdraw to Nantwich. In spite of the winter season, Byron went on the offensive. On 13 December Captain Sandford surprised and captured Beeston Castle with eight firelocks. The Royalist army marched on and began to besiege Nantwich in bitterly cold and snowy weather, but a relief force under Sir Thomas Fairfax was mobilised. The subsequent Battle of Nantwich, on 25 January, shattered the Royalist army, which fell back on Chester. Nantwich was relieved.

The defeated army was billeted on a discontented populace. Although the cavalry led by Colonel Marrow, which had escaped from Nantwich, remained active and conducted a series of raids against the Parliamentary garrisons stationed in villages between Chester and Nantwich, the position of Chester and the North had become

80 *Sir William Brereton, MP for Cheshire and commander of the Parliamentary forces in the county.*

critical. The King sent an expedition led by his nephew, Prince Rupert of the Rhine, who fought a whirlwind campaign through Cheshire and Lancashire. He entered Chester on 11 March and inspected the fortifications, the mayor, Randle Holme II, energetically carrying out the improvements he suggested.[10] A section of the line was cut off, thus shortening the length to be defended; the rest was raised to above head height and a great trench was cut to move cannon behind the defences. The trench still survives as Rock Lane. Having secured Cheshire and Lancashire, Rupert marched his army to relieve York, but on 2 July he was heavily defeated at Marston Moor by the combined armies of English Parliamentarians and Scots Covenanters. He fell back on Chester to recuperate before returning to the King's headquarters at Oxford. The remainder of the summer saw a series of raids against the other side's quarters and in August the energetic Colonel Marrow was killed at Sandiway near Northwich. By the end of the summer Chester was in a more exposed position than before.

81   John, Lord Byron, the Royalist governor of Chester.

From November 1644 the city endured its first period of serious siege. Brereton established a ring of garrisons in the villages around Chester and this initiated another round of night raids. Parties from Chester attacked the isolated forces in Tattenhall, Aldford and Barrow. An attack on 24 January 1645 on the larger garrison at Christleton, three miles east of Chester, was itself ambushed and beaten back to the city with losses. The Parliamentary chronicler records that 'the common soldiers were most of them Chester men, as shoemakers, cobblers, tailors, barbers and the

82   The medieval bridge over the Dee between Holt and Farndon which the Parliamentary soldiers forced in November 1643 in order to cut the road from Chester to North Wales.

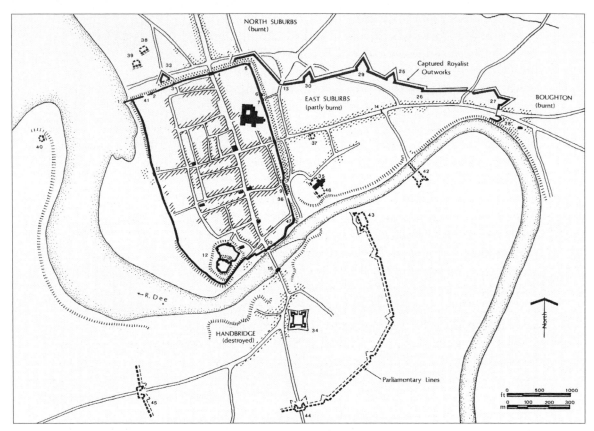

83 *Plan of the outworks in 1644-6 in the later stages of the Civil War.*

like'.[11] In February 1645 a new relief force was mobilised, commanded by Rupert's brother, Prince Maurice. He raised the siege on 19 February and inspected the mud walls, again recommending their shortening. The suburbs outside the North Gate were pulled down and a new mount, called Morgan's Mount, was built outside the North Wall. Only the eastern suburbs and the old walled city were now held. The Chester garrison took the opportunity to push the Parliamentarians out of Christleton and burn down the village, but the siege was resumed as soon as Maurice left. In May the approach of the King's army forced Brereton to lift the siege again, but having reached the borders of Cheshire the King turned his army east across the Midlands and was eventually defeated at Naseby on 14 June. Chester was left undisturbed through the summer and Byron used the time to construct the 'Royal Mount', a fort in Handbridge devised to defend the further end of the bridge.

On the night of 20 September Parliamentary forces secretly assembled outside the eastern outworks. They surprised the guard in one of the mounts, opened the gates and poured into the suburbs. The garrison was alerted and desperate fighting ensued around the Bars. The mayor, Charles Walley, woke to find Parliamentary soldiers in the garden of his house by the Bars and fled up Foregate Street in his nightshirt, just getting through the East Gate before it was closed. The Parliamentary soldiers found the city's ceremonial sword and mace in Mayor Walley's house and sent them down to Parliament. They had captured the suburbs but failed to break into the old city defended by walls. Cannon were brought up to St John's churchyard to bombard the city wall by the New Gate. On 22 September they battered a breach, the evidence for which can still be discerned in the wall fabric. Desperate fighting ensued but the Royalists repelled attempts to force the breach.

Help was at hand. King Charles was at Chirk when he received the news from Chester. He arrived in the city with his Life Guard on 23 September and lodged at the house of Sir Francis Gamull in Lower Bridge Street. The accompanying cavalry, under Sir Marmaduke Langdale, crossed the River Dee at Farndon and bivouacked around Saighton. They planned to crush the Parliamentarian forces in the suburbs the following morning but Colonel General Poyntz, who was trailing King Charles, rode overnight from Whitchurch to assist the Parliamentarians at Chester. His force of cavalry met up with Langdale's at Milners Heath by Waverton and the series of scrappy running fights held on 24 September to the south-east of Chester is known collectively as the Battle of Rowton Moor, the location of the main engagement that afternoon.[12] The result was yet another defeat for the King. He is reputed to have watched the fight from the top of the tower on the city walls that now bears his name but it is more likely he stood on top of the Cathedral Tower, for a captain standing beside him was killed there by an unlucky shot. Casualties were heavy on the King's side and included his cousin, the Earl of Lichfield, and the court composer William Lawes.

84 *Location of the breach in the City Walls near the New Gate unsuccessfully stormed on 22 September 1645.*

King Charles retired into North Wales next day and the siege was resumed. However, Byron had managed to reinforce the garrison with soldiers from Wales. The besiegers brought up more cannon and the gun in Morgan's Mount was destroyed. A second breach was battered in the north side of the city walls on 9 October but again the attacks were beaten back. The women of Chester played a heroic part in digging and bringing up materials to block the breach, several being killed. A French volunteer who called himself the Compte de St Pol distinguished himself with his sword, fencing in defence of the breach dressed only in his shirt. He had joined the King's army but was marooned in Chester after his horse was killed at Rowton Moor.

The besiegers changed their tactics and, instead of trying to take Chester by storm, decided to bombard and starve it into submission. The city north of the river was closely blockaded and new siege lines were dug on the Handbridge side. To aid communication and reinforcement between the Parliamentary forces, a bridge of boats was constructed across to the meadows and

85 *Sir Marmaduke Langdale, commander of King Charles' cavalry at the Battle of Rowton Moor.*

supported by an earthwork fort.[13] The winter of 1645-6 was desperately hard for the citizens and garrison. The city, the walls and the mills were bombarded almost nightly. Many buildings were destroyed and the inhabitants took to living in their cellars. Some of the badly equipped Welsh soldiers froze to death whilst on guard duty. Food ran short and searches were made to prevent hoarding. Lord Byron had to let citizens watch him eating meals in order to demonstrate that he fared no better than anyone else. Randle Holme III, the son of the mayor of 1643-4, has left a graphic account of the damage and suffering.[14]

Eventually, Mayor Charles Walley and the citizens forced Lord Byron to negotiate a surrender.[15] Walley had already been in secret communication with Sir William Brereton, who was using his house in Foregate Street as headquarters.[16] The city capitulated on 3 February 1646. Lord Byron and his troops, less their weapons, were allowed to march out to Conwy. Following the siege, Chester was in a poor state.[17] The royalist corporation was deposed and one sympathetic to Parliament installed in its stead. The bishopric was abolished and the Bishop's Palace plundered. Church ministers were replaced by Presbyterian ones. Many leading Royalists had to pay fines for delinquency. Buildings were badly damaged, most of the suburbs having been demolished, trade was disrupted and the citizenry were exhausted and impoverished. During 1647-8 a severe outbreak of plague killed 2,000 people and the city was deserted. 'God's Providence House' in Watergate Street was, reputedly, the only house which escaped the plague. The mud wall outworks were levelled but plans to demolish the city walls were never carried out. In the abortive Royalist risings of 1648 and 1651, the city, firmly garrisoned by Parliamentary troops, was hardly involved. Following the Earl of Derby's failed attack on Wigan during Charles II's Worcester campaign, the Earl and two others were sentenced to death.[18] Sir Timothy Featherstonhaugh was beheaded in the Market Square outside the Abbey Gate.

The citizens of Chester might have been dismayed by the rule of the Protectorate but they were also desirous of peace and security. Charles Walley even served as the city's MP in Cromwell's Parliament. In 1655 an abortive plot to seize the castle led to the arrests of disillusioned former Parliamentary supporters, including Colonel John Booth who had held Warrington for Brereton. In 1659, after Cromwell's death, a new Royalist rebellion was hatched. Sir George Booth of Dunham Massey (Colonel John's nephew), a Presbyterian and former Parliamentarian, was prepared to support it and was appointed leader in Cheshire. Inevitably the government discovered the plot and the rising was called off, but Booth did not hear until too late. The Royalist gentry rose to support him and so did many former Parliamentarians. John Booth entered

86 *The house of Sir Francis Gamull, where King Charles stayed on 23 and 24 September 1645. The house has had a brick frontage added but the hall inside is much as it was in the 17th century.*

Chester and the mayor and council declared their support, but the castle, held by Colonel Croxton and well supplied and manned, stood against them, making Chester untenable. The rebels moved east but were cornered at Winnington Bridge near Northwich on 19 August by the New Model Army and were utterly defeated. In the following days large numbers of the gentry were arrested, including Sir George Booth who was found disguised as a lady.[19] As punishment, Chester's charter was dissolved, but it was restored within the year and all the prisoners released, and the Restoration of Charles II was greeted with relief and rejoicing.

87 *'God's Providence House' in Watergate Street, reputed to be the only house to escape the outbreak of plague in 1647-8.*

Chapter 7

Polite Society

The later part of the 17th century was marked by a slow recovery and rebuilding after the damage suffered during the Civil War. Rarely would Chester occupy the national stage as prominently as it had done previously. However, in 1682 the authorities in London were alarmed by the progress through Staffordshire and Cheshire of the Duke of Monmouth, illegitimate son of Charles II but a Protestant and preferred by many to the legitimate heir, the King's Catholic brother James. Ostensibly the visit was to attend the races in Wallasey, but the Duke was entertained by many gentry supporters and followed by a great rabble crying, 'a Monmouth, a Monmouth'. He entered Chester on 9 September and stayed with the mayor, George Mainwaring, at his house in Watergate Street. Next day, Sunday, he attended services at the cathedral, stood godfather to the mayor's daughter and dined at the *Plume of Feathers*, Bridge Street. On Monday he set out for Wallasey where he won a silver cup. He did not return to Chester but went instead to Dunham Massey, near Runcorn, the home of Lord Delamere or George Booth, the noted Presbyterian leader of the abortive rising in 1659.[1] The silver cup and the winning horse did return to Chester and were paraded through the streets to great acclaim. In the absence of the Duke, the mob amused themselves by breaking into churches and ringing the bells. They threw stones through the cathedral's stained glass windows and tore up the clergy's vestments.[2] The moment passed, however, and after his accession James II visited the city in 1687. He stayed at the Bishop's Palace but attended a private Catholic mass in the castle chapel. William III visited Chester in 1690.

In 1715, and again in 1745, the Jacobite risings caused alarm. Chester avoided direct involvement but the militia was called out and troops were stationed at the castle. After the Battle of Preston in 1715, 500 Jacobite prisoners were incarcerated in the castle and gaol, where many died of cold and disease. Bonnie Prince Charlie's invasion in 1745 was a greater scare. The city gates were blocked and the citizens instructed to stock up for a two-week siege. The Lord Lieutenant, Lord Cholmondeley, repaired the castle and built gun batteries in each ward (the one in the inner ward still survives).[3] To provide a clear field of fire, he demolished the upper stage of the tower of St Mary's church. Noted military architect Alexander de Lavaux drew up an ambitious scheme to surround the castle with a modern bastion fort, as well as a plan of Chester, one of the earliest accurate surveys we have. In the event, Chester was spared. The Jacobite army marched via Manchester and Derby before retreating to Scotland.

For most of the time, however, Chester enjoyed the life of a prosperous county market town. The buildings destroyed in the Civil War were rebuilt, initially in traditional black and white timber framing. 'Cowper House' in Bridge Street was the home of Thomas Cowper, mayor in 1641, and a beam on the front bears the initials 'TC' and the date 1664. The continued use of timber indicates its availability in the area as well as an old-fashioned taste, as new materials and new styles were making themselves felt. In 1671, following the Great Fire of London, the Assembly decreed that all new houses in the four main streets should henceforth have roofs of tile or slate rather than flammable thatch or shingles. Existing buildings had to conform by All Saints Day. Gamul House in Lower Bridge Street was given a brick frontage, although the medieval open hall behind it was retained.[4] George Booth (grandson of the earlier George) claimed in 1700 to have rebuilt two old houses in Watergate Street to form a fine new town house. In fact, much of the medieval fabric survived.[5] Booth added a

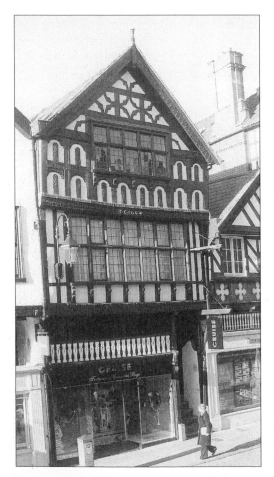

fine brick frontage, with Tuscan columns on the row and a prominent baroque cornice at eaves level, but the rhythm of the windows was spoiled by the retained medieval walls behind. The frontage projected into the street and was angled so that one got a fine view of it from the Cross. Booth's ostentation, however, cost him £10, the fine for encroaching into the street. After his death the house served for much of the 18th century as the city's Assembly Rooms, where fashionable balls and entertainments were held.[6]

In Lower Bridge Street, a more significant change occurred. In 1643, during the siege, Sir Richard Grosvenor, who had moved his family and household into the city from his estate at Eaton, had been allowed to enlarge his house, the Falcon, by enclosing the Row in front of it. This opened the way for a succession of enclosure applications down the street, which peaked in the first quarter of the 18th century.[7] Some enclosures retained the old building and just infilled the row with

88 *Cowper House, the home of Thomas Cowper, in Bridge Street.*

89 *Inscription on Cowper House recording rebuilding work following Civil War damage.*

timber framing, such as the Old Kings Head, Randle Holme's house. Others were completely new buildings. Foremost was the Oddfellows Hall, built as Bridge House by Lady Calveley as 'a grace and ornament' to the city in 1676.[8] It was the first house in Chester built in the neo-classical style. More fine, classical-style mansions followed on the other side of Lower Bridge Street: no. 51, a lawyer's residence, in 1700, and Park House (more recently the Talbot) in 1715. But the historic commercial core of the city retained its Rows, and rebuilding was piecemeal and restricted by the cramped sites, and often confined merely to refacing older buildings in the Georgian style.

New developments were on sites around the periphery of the commercial core. Fine town houses in the eastern suburbs were Dee House, built for the wealthy merchant and mayor, James Comberbach, in around 1730, and the Old Palace overlooking the river, built for Bishop Peploe by 1745. Adjacent to the cathedral lay Abbey Court, which had once housed the brew and bakehouses and store buildings of the old abbey. By this time, however, to the embarrassment of the Dean and Chapter, it was occupied by disreputable alehouses and other unsavoury occupants. From the 1750s these were swept away and Abbey Square, a fine square of Georgian houses suitable

90 *Booth Mansion in Watergate Street was built in 1700 with a modern baroque-style front but in fact retains much of its medieval fabric.*

91 The Falcon *in Lower Bridge Street, home of Sir Richard Grosvenor, was the subject of the first recorded instance (in 1643) of a petition to enclose the Row. The Row walkway still survives within the building.*

for professional gentlemen, was laid out. On the western side of the city there was still much undeveloped land, the former precincts of the dissolved medieval friaries. It was acquired by the Irish Linen Hall proprietors and during the 1780s the Georgian terraces of Stanley Place, Watergate Street Flags and Nicholas Street were laid out. Sedan House on Stanley Place retains a sedan porch, its opposed side entrances allowing a sedan chair to pass through whilst its occupant dismounted under cover. The Nicholas Street terrace acquired the name 'Pillbox Row' from the number of doctors who occupied it.[9]

92 The Old King's Head *in Lower Bridge Street, home of Randle Holme II, mayor in 1643-4, and his son Randle Holme III, the antiquarian.*

93 *Bridge House in Lower Bridge Street, built by Lady Calveley in 1676, was the first neo-Classical building in Chester.*

The civic amenities developed in parallel with the genteel housing. The Exchange was built in Market Square in Northgate Street in 1695-8 to serve as the common hall. The lower floor was open and the main rooms on the first floor were supported on pillars. In 1712 a life-sized statue of Queen Anne was placed in a niche on the front elevation. The open lower floor was used as a market and also contained a coffee house. The mayor still occupied the Pentice, the building wrapped around the south and east faces of St Peter's, at the Cross. The eastern arm was pulled down in 1781 to widen Northgate Street and the rest followed in 1803 when the functions it housed were moved up to the Exchange.

94 *Georgian terraces in Abbey Square dating from c.1760.*

95   *The sedan porch on Sedan House, at the corner of Stanley Place. The porch had opposing doors to enable a sedan chair to be carried through and the occupant to alight under cover.*

It was during this period that the politics and affairs of the city became dominated by the Grosvenor family.[10] In 1677 Sir Thomas Grosvenor, whose family seat at Eaton lay just south of Chester, married a wealthy London heiress. Thereafter he and his descendants expanded their influence and property holdings both in the city and their estate to its south. They led the Tory faction, but elections for the aldermen, the mayor and for Members of Parliament were frequently vigorously contested by the Whigs. Each side tried to pack the body of freemen entitled to vote with their supporters. At the mayoral election in 1732 a riot broke out in Bridge Street, the factions reinforced by disguised soldiers and Liverpool sailors (for the Whigs) and Welsh miners (for the Tories). The mayor called in dragoons from Warrington to restore order and the Tories won the election. Until 1829 the Grosvenor nominations generally held both Parliamentary seats and their faction dominated the Assembly.

96   *The Exchange, built in 1695-8. The ground floor was originally open but was subsequently infilled because of structural concerns. The statue of Queen Anne was added in 1712.*

97 *The Goblin Tower, rebuilt as Pemberton's Parlour at the beginning of the 18th century.*

The city walls had outlived their defensive importance, in spite of the Jacobite scares, but, unlike those in many other cities, they were not pulled down. Instead they were converted to a popular and fashionable perambulation, where people could meet and enjoy views of the town and over the river to the Welsh hills. The wall walk was repaved and several towers were reconstructed to form viewing points and resting stops. The plaque on Pemberton's Parlour (the former Goblin Tower) records the expenditure by the Assembly in 1707 of £1,000 to repair and reflag the walls. The medieval gate towers now obstructed both the traffic entering the city and the perambulation along the wall walk so they were gradually replaced by wide elegant arches surmounted by balustraded parapets. The East Gate went first in 1768. The Bridge Gate followed in 1781 and the Water Gate in 1788, their new arches being designed by Joseph Turner, a local architect and member of the Assembly. Finally, the North Gate containing the notorious city gaol was replaced in 1808-10 and a new gaol built overlooking the Roodee.

98 *The inscription on Pemberton's Parlour records repairs to the walls in 1707 and the paving of 1,000 yards of the walkway for a cost of £1,000 and upwards.*

99 *The East Gate, rebuilt as an elegant arch in 1768.*

The medieval streets remained but were smartened up with new names. What had always been lanes now became streets. Cow Lane changed to Frodsham Street, Parsons Lane to Princess Street and Barn Lane became King Street.

The medieval castle was also obsolete, though it still maintained a garrison and housed the Shire Hall where the exchequer courts were held.[11] In 1696-8 it temporarily housed a mint for the recoinage of William III, the comptroller being Edmund Halley, the famous astronomer. After the Jacobite rebellions had been crushed, less effort was made to maintain it. A large section of the inner bailey wall fell down and was rebuilt in 1760-86, but by the 1780s the condition of the accommodation was very poor and a competition was held to design improvements. Thomas Harrison, an architect then of Lancaster, won, and in 1788 commenced the reconstruction which produced 'one of the most powerful monuments of the Greek Revival in the whole of England'.[12] In a project lasting until 1815, the whole of the outer bailey was

100 *The Bridge Gate, rebuilt in 1781.*

101   *Old Lamb Row at the southern end of Bridge Street. This building had become increasingly dilapidated, and in 1821 the frontage suddenly collapsed. The remains were cleared when Grosvenor Street was laid out. The tower of St Bridget's church rises behind.*

rebuilt. The Shire Hall occupied the central range with a massive central pediment supported by 12 monolithic Doric columns. On either side were flanking wings, the one on the left housing the barracks and the one on the right the armoury. To the front lay a large semi-circular parade ground extending far beyond the old castle bailey. The main entrance was realigned from the north-east to the north-west and was dignified by the 'propylaea' based on the Acropolis in Athens.

The new Shire Hall was a magnificent semi-circular chamber with a domed roof. Behind the new building, and making use of the lower level running down to the river, Harrison built a new gaol, designed on the panoptic principle with the chapel and gaoler's house above in the centre. It was considered the model of a modern and humane prison.[13] The gaol yard extended across the City Wall, a section of which, including the Ship Gate, was demolished. The wall-walk was diverted onto the riverside promenade as far as the Bridge Gate.

The other major institution in the city, the cathedral, was also showing signs of age and neglect. Its income had not increased since the time of Elizabeth and the clergy frequently held profitable benefices elsewhere. Bishop Gastrell (1714-25) lived in Oxford during the whole of his occupation of the see. The deanery and canons' houses were let out to rent, their intended occupants staying at inns on their occasional visits to the city. The cathedral fabric was dilapidated and at the end of the 17th century the south cloister walk had collapsed. Apparently the choir

102 *The outer bailey of Chester Castle was rebuilt in the Greek Revival style by architect Thomas Harrison in 1788-1815. The medieval Inner Bailey can be seen on the right.*

did not impress, either. In 1741 George Handel, on his way to Ireland for the first performance of his *Messiah*, was delayed by bad weather in Chester. He used the opportunity to run through some of the choruses with volunteers from the choir, but the singing was so poor that Handel flew into a rage.[14] Modest repairs and repaving of the church continued through the 18th century, but by its end the fabric was causing considerable concern. In 1818 Thomas Harrison was engaged to survey it. He estimated that a sum of £7,000 was required and a public appeal was launched by Bishop Law. Harrison carried out repairs which included the restoration of the south face of the south transept. The elaborately decorated 14th-century gable wall was replaced by a plain and severe one. However, the leading exponent of the Classical Revival fell out with the cathedral over supervision of the work and withdrew from the commission.

In the 18th century, travel to Dublin was still an important element of Chester's economy, although embarkation usually took place at Parkgate further down the Wirral coast. The silting of the Dee continued to hinder trade and ships found access to the city quays increasingly difficult. Various abortive projects were proposed until a scheme by Nathaniel Kinderley received Parliamentary approval in 1732.[15] In 1735-6 a straight channel, the 'New Cut', was dug on the south side of the old channel from just below Chester to Connahs Quay. It was 16 feet deep and could take vessels up

103 *Thomas Harrison, architect of the Castle, the Grosvenor Bridge and other Classical Revival buildings in Chester.*

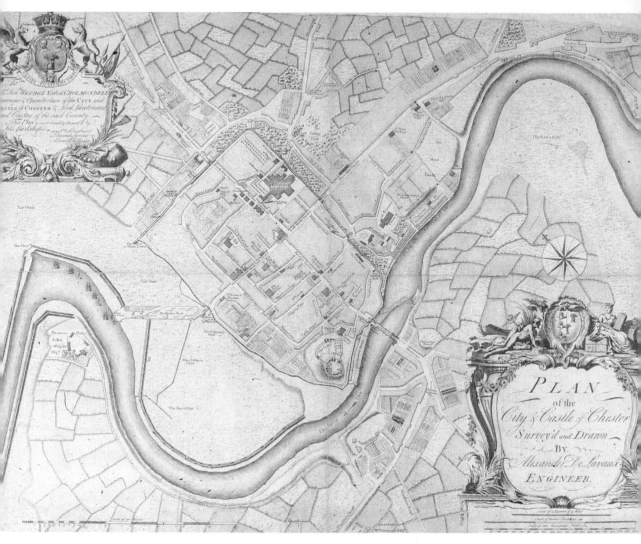

104 *Alexander de Lavaux' plan of Chester of 1745, showing the River Dee flowing through the new cut. Otherwise the city has not developed greatly since the Middle Ages, with little expansion outside the walls except on the east side.*

to 200 tons. In 1740 the proprietors were formed into the River Dee Company. They subsequently received much criticism for their failure to maintain the navigation and for making large profits from reclaimed farmland.

In the early 19th century the city's leaders became aware of a threat posed by the development of the new road (the A5) via Shrewsbury to Holyhead, which provided a much shorter sea crossing. In order to restore the importance of the North Wales coast road a new bridge was required at Chester to supplement the old, narrow, medieval bridge. In 1818 a public meeting was held and a committee chaired by Alderman George Harrison (no relation to the architect) was elected. As well as commissioning Thomas Harrison to design the bridge, he sought the advice of Marc Isambard Brunel

105 *Thomas Harrison's model to demonstrate his design for the new Grosvenor Bridge.*

106 *Construction of the Grosvenor Bridge in 1831.*

107 *View of Nicholas Street, with the new St Bridget's church designed by Thomas Harrison; his rebuilt castle is in the background.*

and Thomas Telford.[16] In 1825 an Act of Parliament was obtained to erect a bridge and its associated approach roads.

Thomas Harrison's plans were for a single-span masonry bridge, 200 feet wide, which was then the widest in the world.[17] There was concern that it would not stand, so he had a model constructed using stone blocks of the correct scale size. The new bridge lay some 600 yards downstream from the old bridge and required the construction of a new approach road. This was the first major departure from the city's medieval street pattern, cutting diagonally from the end of Bridge Street south-westwards past the new castle entrance, through the city walls and across the Roodee on an embankment. Various properties, including old St Bridget's church, would have to be demolished and the land purchased. Earl Grosvenor donated the part he owned to the scheme. A new St Bridget's church was built opposite the castle and consecrated in 1829. Thomas Harrison, by then in his eighties, resigned his position in 1826. He died in 1829 and was buried in a vault in the new St Bridget's churchyard. Few men have done as much to change and dignify

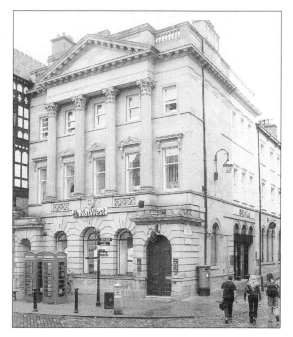

108 *The Chester Bank, Eastgate Street, built 1859-60, was the last major building project in Chester built in the Classical style.*

the face of Chester as he achieved in his lifetime. The work was completed by his student William Cole. Princess Victoria opened the new bridge in 1832 (although it was not finished until the following year), naming it the Grosvenor Bridge. The new approach road became Grosvenor Street and it was equipped with gas lighting.

The new style of Georgian architecture did not sit well within the medieval Rows. Many old buildings were refronted in brick with sash windows but retained their ancient fabric behind. The results were not always satisfactory, as attested by names such as 'Broken Shin Row' and 'The Dark Row'. Enclosure of the Rows in less commercially active areas such as the north side of Watergate Street continued and replacement of buildings continued in a piecemeal fashion. Thomas Harrison built the Commercial Coffee Room, later the Commercial Newsroom, in 1808 on Northgate

Street in his favoured Classical style. It substituted an open street-level arcade for the row. In 1859-60 new premises for the Chester Bank (now the NatWest Bank) were built in Eastgate Street. The building enclosed the Row (with its disreputable reputation) and was built in a bold, prominent Classical style, but caused controversy because the 'black and white' 17th-century timber-framed style had by then regained popularity. The rebuilding of the 1652 'God's Providence House' in Watergate Street in 1862 was acclaimed by the newly established Archaeological Society as a model of conservation. In fact, it was a more or less total rebuild with some of the old timbers reused.

The Gothic Revival which swept through Chester in the second half of the 19th century completed the creation of the appearance and character of the city as it is today.

109 *'God's Providence House', Watergate Street, as restored in 1862. It was, in fact, more or less completely rebuilt.*

Chapter 8

Industry, Workers and Shoppers

During the 18th century Chester gained a reputation as a pleasant place to visit and to shop in, and by the 19th century it was firmly established that the city's face was its fortune. Redevelopment of the main streets in the 1850s witnessed the initially timid start of the black and white revival, but the exuberant late-Victorian Gothic was soon to vanquish completely the popular Classical style and it still dominates Chester's streetscapes. The new style adopted and exploited the medieval Rows and the taste for fashionable shopping and tourism and is nowhere better illustrated than at the famous department store of Browns of Chester on Eastgate Street. In the late 18th century, Messrs William and Henry Brown, silk mercers and milliners, were held in high repute and their store gained a reputation in the 19th century as the Harrods of the North. It was rebuilt in 1828 in the Classical style, but when the store expanded into the neighbouring premises in 1858 the architect Thomas Penson rebuilt them in full Victorian Gothic.[1] He restored and incorporated the medieval 'crypt' or undercroft into his new building. The grandly named 'Architectural, Archaeological and Historic Society of Chester and North Wales', founded in 1849, fully supported this nostalgia for and revival of Chester's traditional architecture. Penson and his fellow architects, James Harrison (no relation to Thomas), Thomas Lockwood and particularly John Douglas, transformed the street frontages of the city with their black and white buildings. The iconic building group at the Cross was designed by Lockwood in 1888.

Chester remained a centre for local government and justice. The prosperous retailers and the developments they supported depended on the city's traditional sources of income, particularly the gentry classes in the surrounding countryside and the professional and service sectors. The great industrial expansion of the 19th century did not make much impact on Chester.[2] Society was still led by the Grosvenor family, which dominated the Assembly. In 1807 the family switched its allegiance to the Whigs over the issue of Catholic emancipation. After 1829 Earl Robert Grosvenor ceased to nominate both of the city's parliamentary candidates, and the 1835 Municipal Corporations Act regularised the election of councillors and aldermen and removed much of the old factionalism and interest. However, the Grosvenors' wealth, property and status continued to grow. Robert, the 2nd Earl, became Marquess of Westminster in 1831. Hugh Lupus, the 3rd Marquess, was elevated to Duke of Westminster in 1874. Throughout the period the family remained patrons and benefactors of numerous civic and charitable projects.

The expansion of the retail and tourist trade was encouraged by improvements in the transport network. In the late 17th century it had taken four days to reach London by stagecoach (six in winter). By 1780, after the introduction of turnpiked roads, it took only two, and travellers were catered for by a growing number of hotels. The *White Lion* in the Market Square was the most famous, but congestion in the city centre led to the development of

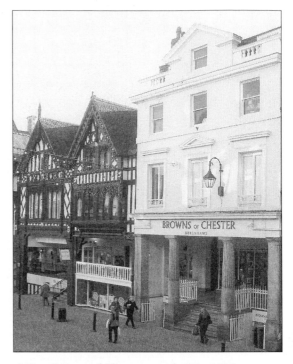

110 *Browns of Chester was rebuilt in 1828 in the still fashionable Classical style.*

inns on Foregate Street (the *Golden Lion*) and Bridge Street (the *Feathers*).[3] The *Royal Hotel* just inside the East Gate was the headquarters of the Independent (anti-Grosvenor) faction until Earl Grosvenor bought it in 1815. As the *Grosvenor Hotel*, it developed into the city's premier place to stay. The present building dates from the 1860s. The tourist trade was also served by a growing quantity of literature, the *Stranger's Handbook to Chester* by Thomas Hughes being published in 1856 and running to many editions.

In 1779, the Chester to Nantwich Canal opened. It ran through a dramatic cutting immediately outside the north walls of the city and joined the Dee by a flight of five locks. The task and cost of making the cutting was much reduced when engineers found they were following the line of the Roman ditch. The canal was not a

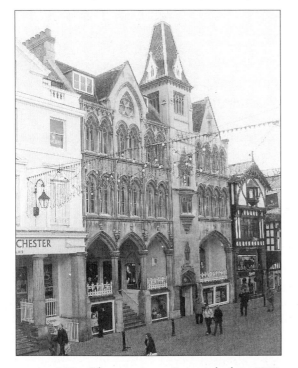

111 *The extension to Browns, built in 1858 in Gothic Revival style.*

112 *The Chester to Nantwich Canal in Boughton, on the outskirts of Chester. It was wide enough to accommodate Mersey flats.*

commercial success, however, for it did not connect with the national network. That only happened in 1795 when the Wirral Line extended the canal to the Mersey at what became Ellesmere Port. This was a greater success and cheese a notable commodity that was carried. A passenger packet also ran to Liverpool. A new basin with boat yard and locks was built at the point where the canal joined the Dee. In 1806 the Ellesmere Canal extended the network to the industrial areas of north-east Wales and finally, in 1833, a link to the Trent and Mersey Canal at Middlewich was dug. The success of the canal sounded the death knell for the port of Chester for it was now easier for goods to continue past Chester to the Mersey and Liverpool.[4]

113 *The canal boat dry dock at the boat yard and Dee Basin were constructed in 1795.*

114 *Chester General Railway Station, built by Thomas Brassey in 1848.*

In the 1820s there were disputes between the Canal Company and River Dee Commissioners regarding tolls and the taking of water from the river which were invariably settled in favour of the canal. In fact, the directors and shareholders of the Canal Company, the River Dee Company (responsible for maintaining the navigation) and the Commissioners were generally one and the same group of people and it was in their interests to promote the profits of the canal. In 1827 the tolls on the canal were drastically increased, and a surcharge for goods travelling a short distance penalised those loaded at Chester. Joseph Swanwick led a campaign by Chester traders to divert their goods back onto the Dee, leasing wharfage and bringing Mersey flats onto the river to carry their goods around the coast. It had the desired effect, and the Canal Company reduced some of the new charges. The Chester traders went back to the canal, much to Swanwick's disgust,[5] but reviving the trade on the river was a lost cause by this time. The River Dee Company succeeded in making large profits but it was by reclaiming the rich area of farmland known as Sealand rather than through maintaining the navigation.

The railways arrived in 1840 when lines to Birkenhead and Crewe were opened. They met on the low-lying land to the north-east of the city at Flookersbrook, where the first station was erected. The line was quickly extended around the city towards Holyhead and Shrewsbury. It tunnelled under Further Northgate Street, crossed the canal by a bridge and cut through the corner of the city walls by the Water Tower. It was raised on a brick viaduct across the Roodee and a new bridge carried it over the Dee. On 24 May 1847, one of the cast-iron girders of the bridge fractured as the Chester to Ruabon train passed over it.[6] The engine made it across but the tender derailed and the fireman was thrown out and killed. The coaches plunged into the river, killing the guard and two passengers. Most of the remaining passengers were severely injured and one later died. The driver bravely drove the engine back across the bridge on the remaining track and returned to Chester station to raise the alarm. The Inquiry found that the construction of cast-iron girders with wrought-iron stays was not sufficiently strong. The bridge was rebuilt and by 1850 the line was open all the way to Holyhead.

The rapid expansion of the railways increased the number of visitors to Chester and a proper station building appropriate to the dignity of the city was thought necessary. It opened in 1848 and had an immensely long Italianate-style frontage. The building contractor was the locally born Thomas Brassey. He was to become the foremost railway engineer of his age, constructing railway lines around the world. A new approach road to the station, City Road, was opened in 1860 to link the station directly with Foregate Street and the city centre. The *Queen Hotel* opposite the station was built in the 1860s to serve travellers by rail.

The public buildings of Chester were also rebuilt or restored. The Exchange in the Market Square was gutted by fire in 1862 although, fortunately, the city's ancient

115 *The interior of the Railway Station.*

archives and many pictures were rescued. There followed a competition to design a new Town Hall. This was built on a large site on the west side of Market Square and was opened in 1869 by the Prince of Wales accompanied by Prime Minister Gladstone. It contained the Council Chamber, Magistrates Court and Assembly Rooms. In the basement were cells and the police station. The old produce markets were also cleared from the middle of Market Square and housed in a purpose-built Market Hall opened in 1863 alongside the site of the new Town Hall. The Exchange fire also exposed the inadequacies of the city's fire-fighting arrangements and a new force, the Earl of Chester's Volunteer Fire Brigade, was formed. The City Council provided a fire station on Northgate Street and in 1874 bought their first steam-powered fire engine.

116 *The Victorian Old Market Hall, built 1863, on the left, and Town Hall, built 1869, on the right, enabled the Market Square to be cleared of buildings.*

Virtually all the city's churches received major restorations in the later 19th century. Chester's red sandstone does not weather well and decay was probably exacerbated by the fumes from the numerous coal fires. St Michael's and Holy Trinity were completely rebuilt. At the cathedral major programmes of restoration resulted in substantial refacing and rebuilding of the exterior. The noted architect Sir George Gilbert Scott worked on the cathedral from 1855 to 1876 and is largely responsible for its external appearance, notably the turrets and pinnacles that adorn it.[7]

The 18th and 19th centuries were times of enormous growth for Chester, as elsewhere. The 1801 population of 15,000 had grown to over 38,000 by the end of the century. The city expanded outside its old boundaries, the middle

117 *The tower at St John the Baptist church collapsed early on Good Friday morning 1881. It had been exhibiting cracks and movement for sometime. The porch, destroyed by falling masonry, was rebuilt but the tower was reduced to a stump.*

118 *The derelict cloisters at Chester Cathedral in 1811. Through the gaping windows of the north cloister walk, devoid of its tracery, may be seen the chambers over the east cloister, themselves in a poor state of repair, which were removed shortly after.*

and professional classes moving away from the main streets into new suburbs along Boughton and also Queen's Park across the river. Although the greatest effects of the industrial revolution passed the city by, and it lost its pre-eminence as the largest settlement in the county to the growing industrial towns of Birkenhead, Macclesfield and Stockport and the new railway town of Crewe, there were many urban poor. They were housed in the courts which packed the formerly open yards and back lands behind the main streets. The courts were often accessed by narrow entries and comprised rows of back-to-back houses. Irregular water supply came from shared standpipes and sanitation was represented by communal earth closets.

119 *Chester Cathedral from the south-east at the end of the 19th century, after completion of the programmes of restoration.*

120 *Posnett's Court behind the south side of Watergate Street.*

There was also a great swathe of terraced housing on the north-east side of the city between Boughton, the canal and the railway. Conditions here were not conducive to good health and there were outbreaks of cholera in 1832, 1849 and 1866. The Chester Royal Infirmary refused to take cholera patients and temporary hospitals were opened on vacant land adjacent to the city. It was clear by now that the water supply and sewerage were completely inadequate for the population. An Improvement Commission had been set up in 1762 and reformed in 1803. It was chaired by the mayor and included such city worthies as JPs, the Recorder and the Dean and Chapter. Its remit covered policing, fire services and street lighting and cleanliness. The reformed commission set about building sewers in most of the main streets but it was only after the middle of the century that the system was extended to Foregate Street, Boughton and the city centre courts. The drains were a great improvement but lacked sufficient water to flush them out properly and the stench in hot weather became unbearable.

121 *Davies Court off Steam Mill Street in Boughton. In the mid-20th century the ten houses shared one tap and four WCs.*

Chester's water supply came from the river and the city's situation on a hill made it difficult to maintain pressure. The water was drawn from near the Dee Bridge in the area where the tides reached their head and the sewage discharged into the river. In 1825 a new waterworks company was formed by Act of Parliament, and a new intake from the river was constructed at Barrel Well Hill, upstream from the weir, in 1828. However, the expanded sewerage system in the 1850s endangered this intake, too, and eventually it was moved upstream and across the river. Contamination remained a cause for concern until the end of the century and was blamed for increases in typhoid.[8] Supply was enhanced by the provision of public fountains, the one at the junction of Grosvenor Street and Bridge Street provided by former mayor Meadows Frost being particularly magnificent.

Another major addition to the city's amenities was the opening of the Grosvenor Park in 1867. An area of farmland and the grounds of the former Cholmondeley Mansion to the east of St John's church were gifted to the city by Richard Grosvenor, 2nd Marquess of Westminster, and laid out as a public park, with John Douglas designing the keeper's lodge. The park extended down to the river, which was lined by the Groves. Walking by the river and boating became favoured pastimes of the period. In 1883 a floating bath was established on the river, but in 1899 it broke from its moorings and got stuck on the weir. It was replaced by the new City Baths in Union Street, adjacent to the Park, which opened in 1901. The frontage of the building was designed, almost inevitably, by John Douglas.

Chester avoided major industrial expansion because of its geographical position and competition from neighbouring Manchester and Liverpool, but there was also opposition (or at least lack of support) from the city's ruling élite.[9] However, the city was not without some industrial enterprises. In 1800 a leadworks was established on the north side of the

122 *Mayor Frost's public fountain at the junction of Grosvenor Street and Bridge Street in the late 19th century. The procession is Barnum and Bailey's street pageant depicting Columbus' return from America.*

canal. It incorporated a shot tower, some 166 feet tall, which still stands and is thought to be the last remaining one in the country. The Napoleonic Wars provided a ready market for its produce. Two steam-powered corn mills were also built on the canal. The Dee Mills burnt down in 1789 and were rebuilt, but burned down again in 1819

123 *Statue of Richard Grosvenor, 2nd Marquess of Westminster, in Grosvenor Park, the land for which he gifted to the city in 1867.*

and were again repaired. They also suffered from competition with the new mills on the canal. The causeway or weir across the river also provided a location for mills on the southern side in Handbridge. In the 18th and 19th centuries they formed the focus for a small industrial area.[10] Traditionally, there had been fulling mills and tanning in this area, and now there grew up paper mills, a pottery and needle manufacturing. But it was snuff and tobacco that would prove the most enduring. In 1845 Thomas Nicholls took over the snuff mills and the company named after him was run by his descendants for more than a century.

The main industrial area of 19th-century Chester grew up to its south-west in Saltney, where the Shrewsbury and Chester Railway built a wharf on the River Dee in 1846. It attracted various industrial enterprises, including Henry Wood and Co., who were chain makers, oil refineries and chemical works. This development was only partly in Chester. It lay mainly across the border in Flintshire and was not therefore so objectionable to the city. The middle decades of the 19th century were prosperous ones but this was not sustained, and by the end of the century most of

124 *Pleasure steamers on the River Dee passing the large villas lining Boughton.*

125   *The lead shot tower from the Chester Leadworks.*

126   *Griffiths' steam-powered corn mill on the canal, shortly before demolition in the 1980s.*

127   *The Old Dee Bridge and Chester viewed from Handbridge in the 19th century, showing the Dee Mills and the rebuilt Bridge Gate. Behind can be seen St Mary's church and the new gaol designed by Thomas Harrison. The chimney to the right of the church is from the gasworks in Cuppin Street.*

128 *Bonewaldesthorne's Tower when it served as the Mechanics Institution museum, seen from the Water Tower. The statue of Queen Anne from the burned-down Exchange stands on the steps, and the camera obscura projects from the tower roof.*

the traditional Chester industries, such as leather working, brewing, linen and shipbuilding, had all but disappeared and the growth of the new ones had not been sustained. The absence of large industrial concerns limited the opportunities for employment and the most common jobs were unskilled labouring on farms, market gardens or the railways. Opportunities for the development of a skilled and better-paid working class were limited and so society in Chester in the second half of the 19th century was marked by extremes. On the one hand, the gentry and better-off professional classes lived in comfortable houses and frequented the smart shops on the main streets. On the other, the urban poor still lived in the overcrowded and unsanitary courts in spite of efforts to ameliorate their conditions.

In 1849 the Reverend William Massie, rector of St Mary's, founded the Chester Architectural, Archaeological and Historical Society. It set out to promote the Gothic Revival in architecture in Chester, in which cause it was remarkably successful. Its interests soon spread to the recording and collecting of antiquities in the city, particularly Roman ones. It also endeavoured to expand its membership beyond the inevitable clergymen and architects by encouraging ladies, young men engaged in the shops and offices, and the industrious and intelligent artisan to join.

In 1870 Charles Kingsley, the author of *The Water Babies, Westward Ho!* and other works, became a canon at the cathedral. He promoted the foundation of the Natural Science Society the following year. The two societies rapidly acquired collections of natural history and

129 *Hugh Lupus Grosvenor, 1st Duke of Westminster, 1825-99, benefactor of the Grosvenor Museum and numerous other projects in Chester.*

130 *Crowds packing Bridge Street during the Chester Cup race day.*

antiquities. Meanwhile, the Chester Mechanics' Institution had developed a museum at the Water Tower and adjoining Bonewaldesthorne's Tower. Attractions included a camera obscura, an observatory and a Roman hypocaust. The collection passed into the ownership of the City Council in 1876 and they, with the two societies, recognised the desirability of opening a proper city museum. Hugh Lupus Grosvenor, 1st Duke of Westminster, presided over an appeal committee in 1883 and donated a plot of land in Grosvenor Street. The museum was built and opened in 1886 as the Grosvenor Museum. In addition to housing the three societies' collections, it contained an art gallery and a school of science and art. It soon needed more space and a new wing was added in 1895. The remarkable Robert Newstead was appointed as curator. He had left school at the age of ten and worked as a gardener but his employer stimulated his interest in natural history and then supported his application for the curatorship. His knowledge of entomology led him to be appointed to a lectureship at Liverpool University in 1905 and to a professorship six years later. Whilst there, he achieved worldwide renown for his work on the tsetse fly and its relationship to African sleeping sickness. He retired in 1924 and returned to Chester as honorary curator. He then established a new career for himself as an archaeologist and carried out many important excavations in the city, his discoveries forming the bedrock of our understanding of Roman Chester. He died, still working, in 1947.

The major entertainment event in the calendar for the whole of the district during this period was the Chester Races. Horse racing had been held on the Roodee since the 16th century under the auspices of the mayor and corporation. The construction of the railway viaduct established the track in the form that has endured today. The main meeting settled down to the first week in May and the major event was the Chester Cup. Grandstands were added and Chester Cup day was soon regarded as a holiday across the region. Huge crowds came to the meetings and the week was eagerly anticipated by the city's traders and publicans. Local divines including Dean Howson and Canon Charles Kingsley warned of the moral dangers of gambling, drunkenness and brawling, but not surprisingly the popularity of the races remained undiminished.[11]

131   *The Royal Agricultural Show held on the Roodee in 1858. The railway viaduct bounds the far side of the Roodee.*

Similar behaviour in the poorer areas of the city was an ongoing concern and frequently blamed on the Irish. Chester had always had a significant Irish element among its population, but in the 19th century St John's parish acquired a large concentration of Irish who were amongst the poorest occupants of the city. During the famine years of the 1840s, large numbers of immigrants settled in the area between Boughton and the canal. Steven Street in particular became notorious in the local press for rowdy and drunken behaviour. The majority of residents were inevitably Roman Catholic and therefore viewed with suspicion. However, their indigent condition also evoked pity. What aid they received was due in no small measure to Father Carberry, the Catholic priest at the Queen Street chapel from 1838-61, who was held in wide respect by the whole city for his charitable work.[12]

A more militant approach to the perceived problem was taken by the Salvation Army and it resulted in the riot of 'Black Sunday', 26 March 1882.[13] Salvationists had become established in Chester the previous year and were soon attracting congregations numbering thousands to their meetings in City Road. They promulgated a message of militant evangelism and strict temperance. In March, General Booth himself visited Chester and a large parade marched him from the station to the city centre. On 26 March the Salvationists formed up again at the end of Boughton to parade into Chester, carrying the banner presented by General Booth and escorted by two police officers, but a large crowd was waiting for them as they turned into Steven Street. The police officer led the way, but as the procession passed it was pelted with missiles. Further assaults and fighting broke out as the Salvationists marched along the canal side and many, including the leader Captain Miriam Falconbridge, were injured. The survivors eventually made it to their meeting hall in City Road. That afternoon a mock parade larger than the mob of the morning formed up, intending to march on the Salvationists' meeting hall, but it was dispersed by police reinforcements.

132   *Steven Street, Boughton, centre of the poor Irish community in the mid-19th century and scene of the 'Black Sunday' riot on 26 March 1882.*

The magistrates subsequently took a balanced and conciliatory view of the events of the day. Those convicted, who had mainly Irish surnames, were bound over to keep the peace. It was recognised that the action of the Salvationists in marching through the strongly Irish and Catholic area had been provocative. It was also acknowledged that strong drink was a factor in the disturbances, which had been planned in the pubs beforehand. The magistrates' policy proved effective and further serious disturbances were avoided. However, a permanently manned police station was opened in Boughton.

The Irish were again the source of alarm in 1866 but this time it was not the local inhabitants. The Fenians in Liverpool, who included numbers of American Irish veterans of the Union army in the American Civil War, hatched a plot to seize the magazine of arms at Chester Castle.[14] They would then commandeer trains to Holyhead, destroying the line behind them, take ships to Dublin and raise insurrection. However, the Fenians were comprehensively penetrated by police informers who, on 10 February, learned that the raid would take place the following day. The garrison,

133 *Grosvenor Street with the* King's Head Inn *where John McCafferty, leader of the Fenian raid, stayed.*

two companies of the 54th Regiment, were put on alert and the following night a further company arrived by train, followed by a battalion of the Fusilier Guards from London sent by the Home Secretary. The Fenians realised they had been betrayed and large numbers were turned back on trains or on ferries from Liverpool, but many did reach Chester and local citizens were bemused by the large number of ruffians aimlessly wandering the streets. Apparently, a quantity of small arms and weapons were dropped into the canal by the station and the pubs in Boughton did a good day's trade. The leader, Captain John McCafferty, never appeared. He had stayed in the *Kings Head* on Grosvenor Street beforehand but laid low on the day. He was subsequently arrested after landing at Dublin and was sentenced to death for treason but he was reprieved. There was concern that soldiers in the garrison may have been suborned and its numbers were increased later in the year.

By the end of the 19th century the traditional Chester industries, tanning and leather working, linen, shipbuilding and related trades, had all died away. The Dee Mills burned down yet again in 1895 and were not rebuilt,[15] and the new industries associated with engineering and the railways endured but did not expand. The city continued to develop, instead, as a centre for service and retail and as a tourist

134 *Chester Horse Fair in Foregate Street, 1877.*

135 *Horse-drawn tram passing the public fountain in Bridge Street. Trams were introduced in 1879. The tram company was bought by the corporation and the trams were electrified in 1903.*

destination. The issue that most exercised the council and citizens at the end of the century was a suitable way to commemorate the Diamond Jubilee of Queen Victoria in 1897. Eventually, the scheme to erect a clock on the East Gate was settled upon. The clock was built by J.B. Joyce of Whitchurch and mounted in a wrought-iron structure designed by John Douglas. It was eventually unveiled in 1899. It has since become the enduring and much photographed icon of the city.

136   *The East Gate with its Jubilee Clock erected in 1899 to commemorate Queen Victoria's Diamond Jubilee in 1897.*

Chapter 9

Modern Chester – the City lost and found

During the 20th century Chester experienced the growth, development pressures and changes common to most urban centres, and this led to debate on what the future character of the city should be. In the middle years of the century the idea of Chester as a historic and architectural gem came to within in an ace of being lost altogether. Fortunately, financial stringency and two world wars retarded the more drastic proposals until wiser counsel could prevail.[1]

At the end of the 19th century the geographical area of the city was expanding through the growth of suburbs. The borough of Hoole had been effectively absorbed but there was still space to be infilled in the immediate environs of the historic city, round Grosvenor Park where Bath Street was built in 1901, and between Boughton, the main road east and the river, where large villas were erected. Curzon Park, to the south-west across the river, remained the most exclusive suburb. Queen's Park to the south-east also expanded, having been connected to the city by a pedestrian suspension bridge in 1852 which was replaced by a new bridge in 1923 after it became unsafe.

To the north-east, in the vicinity of the railways and in Newtown, and to the north-west, in the canal basin area, numerous streets of terraced housing were built in the decades around the turn of the century. The better, later, ones had back yards with outside toilets and an entry onto a back alley. In 1901-4, the first council houses in the city were built on the south side of Tower Road, but the historic city centre behind the main streets and Handbridge over the river were still packed with courts of back-to-back houses where conditions had hardly improved in fifty years. Some work had been done, 20 courts having been cleared by 1894 and a further 30 by 1908, but in the city centre this was an opportunity for commercial expansion and there was little replacement housing. It only exacerbated the overcrowding elsewhere.[2]

On the main streets, retail outlets continued to predominate. On a large prominent site on the east side of Bridge Street, the Duke of Westminster built a new block of shops incorporating an arcade running back from the street at row level. St Michael's Row and Arcade was finished in 1910 in a new style of cream and gold ceramic tiles with baroque motifs.[3] The design was too much for the traditionalists of

137 *The St Michael's Row building, rebuilt in timber framing in 1911 after a public outcry over the design of the previous year. The tiled frontage of the first design still survives on the ground floor.*

Chester, however, and after a storm of protest the Duke took down the Bridge Street façade and replaced it with a traditional, but huge, black and white timber-framed structure. The new St Michael's Arcade survived behind, however, and provides a light and elegant enclosed shopping area. In 1910 a fire at the coach and carriage works on Northgate Street, close to the Town Hall, led to the development of the building as the Westminster Coach and Motor Car Works. The rebuilding was completed by 1914, and the frontage is dominated by richly decorated brick and terracotta tiles. This time, on a site away from the Rows, the design was accepted.[4] It might seem strange to find a motor car manufactory located on a main commercial street, but at this period motor cars were still very much luxury items. At the outbreak of the First World War, Chester was an old-fashioned and declining county town with stagnant or dying industry and only its high quality shopping outlets provided any vibrancy.

The city was the headquarters for Western Command and became the local centre for recruitment and training, for which purpose the army took over the Roodee. When war broke out, the 1st Battalion the Cheshire Regiment was immediately dispatched to France and was almost wiped out at the Battle of Mons. Their stand against two

German corps allowed the rest of the British Expeditionary Force to escape. By the end of the war, the regiment had raised 38 battalions and won two Victoria Crosses.[5] The city's adopted ship, the light cruiser HMS *Chester*, was heavily engaged at the Battle of Jutland on 31 May 1916, and Boy First Class J.T. Cornwell was awarded a posthumous Victoria Cross for his action in the battle. The White Ensign flown by HMS *Chester* in the battle is still lodged in the cathedral. The races and municipal elections were suspended for the duration so Mayor John Frost served until 1919. Several large houses, including Eaton Hall, home of the Grosvenor family, became military hospitals or nursing homes. The population was expanded by war workers, especially at the government munitions factory in Queensferry in Flintshire. The shortage of male workers led the corporation to recruit women as tram conductors and lamp lighters, but they were quickly dismissed at the conclusion of hostilities.[6]

Inevitably, numerous Chester families were bereaved by the war. At its end, the names of 771 Chester citizens who had died in action were placed on a Roll of Honour at the Town Hall. The city also wished to erect a war memorial in a central location but this seemingly straightforward task proved difficult and contentious. Sites in Town Hall Square and at the Cross were rejected because they would be a traffic obstruction. A site on the Cathedral Green on St Werburgh's Street was then identified, and in 1920 Giles Gilbert Scott, the cathedral architect, was asked to provide a design, but the newly installed Dean Bennett rejected the first of these and the war memorial committee rejected the second. Meanwhile, Scott had been dismissed as cathedral

138 *Banner Court off Princess Street, demolished during the 1930s.*

architect due to his numerous other commitments.[7] A public competition was held and a design of a simple 'Cheshire-style' sandstone cross by Royson and Crossley was chosen. The memorial on the Cathedral Green was finally dedicated in 1922.

After the war, Chester's economic and housing problems remained. More council housing was built, particularly on the new estate at the Lache, beyond the suburbs of Curzon Park and Hough Green, and also in Handbridge and on Boughton Heath. However, the council was determined that housing provision should not be a burden on rate payers and the rents made council houses unaffordable for the poorest, to many of whom the notorious courts were still home. It was widely acknowledged that such living conditions had a deleterious effect on health and life expectancy, and the death rate in the slums was nearly double the city's average, which was itself higher than the national average for small towns. Moreover, the water company was still a private enterprise and the purity of the supply remained a cause for concern. In 1932 the council built a new sewage works in Bumpers Lane, well downstream from the city, and this improved the situation. One of the worst areas of courts, around Princess Street and Crook Street, was cleared in the 1930s in spite of vociferous protests. Some of those displaced moved to the new council estates but those unable to afford the rents moved to other highly congested areas off Watergate Street and New Crane Street.

The majority of Chester residents worked in the service sector, which included transport, especially the railways, retail and local administration. The main retail area extended out from Eastgate Street and along Foregate Street, where national high street chains like W.H. Smith and Marks and Spencer became established. Industrial

139 *Swan Court off Foregate Street.*

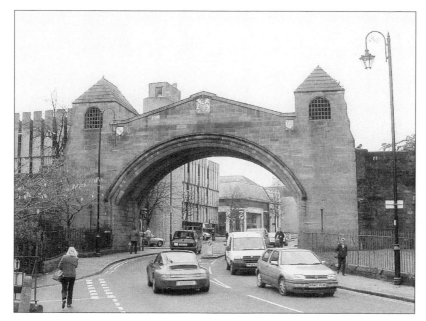

140 *The New Gate opened in 1938. The old gate, known by its old name of Wolf Gate, lies to the north.*

employment was provided by developments in neighbouring areas such as Ellesmere Port and Shotton steelworks in Flintshire. In Chester there remained the Leadworks and a number of newer small-scale engineering concerns, including Williams and Williams on Liverpool Road which made metal window frames.

That manifestation of the modern world, the cinema, reached Chester in 1920, when the first opened in the converted Music Hall. This building has had a remarkable history. Built in the 14th century as a chapel of the abbey, it served in turn as the Common Hall, the Wool Hall, a theatre, a music hall and a cinema. It still stands and is used as a shop. The Odeon was built in 1936 on a very prominent site at the north end of Town Hall Square in typical art-deco style, making a decided contrast to the surrounding Georgian and Victorian buildings. The Regal was built at the same time in Foregate Street.

In the interwar period the city's municipal and parliamentary politics were dominated by the Conservative party. The first female councillor elected in the city was Mrs Phyllis Brown, a member of the Browns of Chester store family. She was elected in 1920 and was a Liberal. She became the first female alderman and, in 1939, the first female mayor. Throughout this time, Mr J.H. Dickson served as town clerk (1903-39) and Charles Greenwood as city engineer and surveyor (1922-53). Although the city was classified as a county borough, it was one of the smallest in the country. The expansion of the suburbs had resulted in a large number of the citizens actually living outside the borough boundaries, so the city lobbied to have the boundaries extended and in spite of opposition from the County Council achieved a moderate expansion in 1936, taking in parts of Blacon, Newton and Hoole.[8]

There was considerable debate at this time about the future direction of the city. The ancient fabric was generally very dilapidated, and although many of the slums in the courts had been cleared little replacement development had occurred, and many old buildings on the Rows were poorly maintained. Should the city become a modern commercial and retail centre, dependent on large industrial concerns in neighbouring areas for employment opportunities, or should it remain a historic town and develop as a tourist destination? For a while it looked like the modernists would win. In 1928 the trams were replaced with motor buses and a period of fierce competition with the local private bus company, Crosville, ensued. Traffic congestion was a serious problem, the main road to the North Wales coast and Holyhead still passing through the city centre and over the Grosvenor Bridge. The old street plan, with the Cross at its centre and the gates through the walls, was not conducive to a smooth traffic flow, but proposals to develop a ring road were largely ignored because of the financial stringencies of the time. However, a scheme to develop an

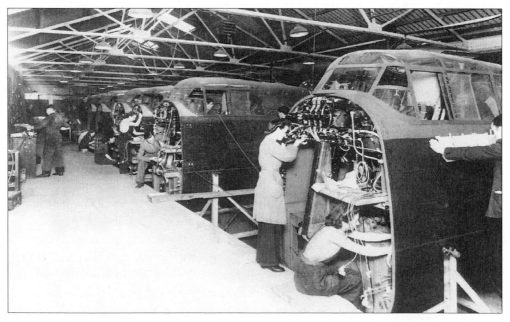

141 *Installing control panels in Wellington bombers at Anchor Motors works. The planes were assembled at the Broughton works.*

142 *The Home Guard parading past the front of the Town Hall.*

alternative route through the south part of the city, improving Vicars Lane and Pepper Street, did progress. It entailed cutting a new gate through the walls and straightening the loop in the road by St John's church, but recent discoveries had just revealed that the loop existed because, from time immemorial, the road had skirted the ruins of the Roman amphitheatre. So the proposal was met by a vociferous counter-campaign to save the amphitheatre led by the Archaeological Society, which even received a letter of support from Mussolini, that guardian of Roman heritage. Sufficient funds were raised to purchase St John's House, which lay over part of the site, and the council was obliged to improve the existing route around the amphitheatre. A cut was made through the City Wall and the 'New Gate' opened in 1938. It was built of sandstone and its design conformed to the generally medieval feel of the walls.

As war clouds gathered and the nation rearmed, the government sponsored the construction of a shadow aircraft factory at Broughton, just over the Welsh border. The factory was operated by Vickers-Armstrong in order to build the Wellington two-engined bomber and was in production in time for the outbreak of war in September 1939.[9] An aerodrome, RAF Hawarden, was opened alongside. The war brought blackouts, rationing and air-raid precautions,[10] but besides housing the headquarters of Western Command, now installed in a large building in Queen's Park, the city hosted

143 *American GIs exploring historic Chester, here at King Charles Tower.*

several army camps. The 22nd Cheshire Regiment was based at the Dale, north of the city. Its strength was raised to seven battalions and they served in most theatres of the war, including France, North Africa, Italy and North-West Europe.[11] Blacon Camp to the north-west of the city carried out machine-gun training, and to the east another training camp lay at Saighton. RAF Sealand was a large base which conducted training and maintenance throughout the war. It was also soon home to a contingent of Polish airmen.

Most of the industrial firms in Chester went over to war work and, with the aircraft factory at Broughton, soon mopped up the city's unemployment. Even very small works produced sections of Wellington bombers which were assembled at Broughton. The motor car works proved particularly suitable, Anchor Motors by the canal near City Road assembling tail units and control panels.[12] In all, 5,540 Wellingtons were completed at Broughton during the war.[13] In 1944 the factory also commenced assembly of Avro Lancasters, a total of 235 being built together with 11 of the improved Lincolns. Williams and Williams turned from window frames to jerry cans, producing several million during the war. They also constructed parts for the top secret Mulberry Harbours used in the invasion of Europe.[14] Another local electrical engineering firm, Brookhirst, produced electrical gear for ships and artillery.

Chester's distance from enemy bases and the lack of major industry meant it was considered a safe town for evacuees. A large number was sent from Manchester and Liverpool, both of which were badly hit by bombing raids, and the evacuees more than doubled the city's school population. Chester suffered only a small number of raids, mainly of incendiary bombs. The worst were on 28 and 29 November 1940. A parachute land mine was hit by anti-aircraft fire and exploded over the city, blowing out a large number of windows including some at the cathedral. The following day the streets were thick with broken glass, but only three people were killed. On 1 January 1941 a raid on the gas works missed its target but demolished houses in Kitchen Street, killing one woman. Two German bombers crashed in the fields around Chester and a crash at Poulton killed all the crew, but at Bumpers Lane the crew survived and were arrested and held at the castle.

As the war progressed, the military bases around Chester proliferated. The Dartmouth Naval College was bombed and so in September 1942 it was moved to Eaton Hall, a small town of nissen huts being built in the Duke's gardens. An airfield which operated as a satellite of Hawarden was also built on the Duke's estate at Poulton. The Americans arrived in 1942 and large camps were set up at Vicars Cross (the rugby club), Hoole Bank House and in Claverton, south of the city. GIs became a familiar sight in the city, exploring the historic scenes and enjoying the local entertainment. They inevitably made an impression on the locals and Chester had its share of GI brides. In June 1944 the camps were suddenly deserted as the invasion of Europe was launched.[15]

144   *The VE Day party in Pitt Street.*

Following the end of the war Chester returned to the problem of deciding which course it wanted to follow. Initially, modern development was promoted and the industrial concerns reverted to their peacetime roles. The Broughton aircraft factory's future was doubtful for a while, but it survived by making prefabricated houses. It was transferred to de Havilland and was soon assembling commercial and military jets. The factory started producing Comet airliners but production was suspended after three of these crashed in service. Once the problems had been resolved, assembly of Comet 4s could continue until 1964, when de Havilland was absorbed into the Hawker Siddeley group. The factory continued to flourish, making Airbus wings as part of BAe systems and Airbus UK.[16]

145 *Construction in 1966 of the St Martin's Way section of the Inner Ring Road, cutting through the city walls and elevated over the canal and railway.*

The older industrial concerns in Chester did not fare so well. Thomas Nicholls & Co., the tobacco works in Handbridge, closed in 1954.[17] The industries on the canal, the Lead Works and grain mills, had all shut down by the mid-1980s. The local firms of Williams and Williams and Brookhirst also closed. But industrial employment was expanded by the growth of major plants in Ellesmere Port and Deeside, many of whose workers chose to live in Chester. The closure of the Shotton Steelworks in 1979, however, was a severe blow. The retail and service sectors remained the main

146 *St Martin's Gate, where the Inner Ring Road passes through the city wall.*

147 *Looking south from St Martin's Gate along the Inner Ring Road.*

driving forces of the local economy. Chester remained the most important shopping centre in the region, providing an attractive and historic environment to visitors. Tourism continued to develop, with increasing numbers of foreign parties, especially Americans, enjoying the historic attractions.

During the 1960s this character was under serious threat. Slum housing was still being cleared from the city centre and immediate environs in the 1950s and replaced by large amounts of council housing on the outer edge of the suburbs, notably the new estate at Blacon on the site of the wartime army base. Nor had the traffic congestion been resolved. The Cross in the centre of the city was still heavily used, even sections of Comet fuselage en route from Belfast to Broughton being manoeuvred round the right-angled corner.[18] The solution was to construct the Inner Ring Road, which carved northwards from the castle and around the west, north and north-eastern parts of the historic centre to the end of City Road. Although it did do much to improve traffic flow, it also destroyed many historic buildings and created a barrier between the centre and the old suburbs. It cut through the northern city walls and a concrete arch, St Martin's Gate, was built to carry the wall walk. The Inner Ring Road was associated with the redevelopment of the cleared area behind the Town Hall. What became known as the Forum was completed in 1972 and incorporated shops, the market, council offices and car parks. Its brick, concrete and glass frontage was particularly unattractive and was immediately unpopular with Cestrians, especially as the fine Victorian façade of the Old Market Hall was demolished to make way for it. Several more office blocks housing government or local authority departments were constructed around the Forum.

The Grosvenor Precinct was built in the opposite quadrant of the city, behind Bridge Street and Eastgate Street, and resulted in a multi-storey car park butting up close to the city walls and another concrete and glass façade along Pepper Street. These developments secured the city's position as a fashionable shopping centre but caused disquiet amongst those concerned about the damage to the city's ancient fabric and character. The construction of car parks and service bays beneath the new developments had destroyed Roman structures such as the elliptical building and bathhouse that had survived below ground till then to a very impressive degree.[19] At the same time, the

148   *Derelict buildings in Lower Bridge Street in 1974. They have since been restored and brought back into use.*

historic buildings on Watergate Street and Lower Bridge Street were falling into a potentially disastrous state of repair.

A shift in public opinion was taking place which would be as significant as that in the previous century which had led to the Gothic Revival. The Chester Civic Trust, founded in 1959, provided a voice for local concerns. The Insall Report, published in 1968 with support from the government, changed the whole thrust of development

149   *The 17th-century Dutch Houses in Bridge Street were saved in the 1970s from dereliction and collapse by the City Council's conservation programme.*

150 *The Roman amphitheatre, excavated and displayed in the 1960s.*

policy in the city.[20] It showed that restoration of old buildings could enhance the economy and desirability of the city and maintain its unique qualities for residents and visitors. In 1969 the whole of the centre was designated a conservation area. Major programmes of restoration improved Bridge Street, Lower Bridge Street and Watergate Street. The Dutch Houses, Bishop Lloyds Palace and the *Falcon* were amongst the buildings saved and brought back into worthwhile use. A major archaeological project was at last undertaken in the 1960s at the Roman amphitheatre, the rents from St John's House having accrued sufficiently for the Archaeological Society to finance a dig supported by government grants. It was directed by Hugh Thompson, then curator of the Grosvenor Museum. The site opened in 1972 as a guardianship monument,[21] and since that date a permanent professional archaeological team has been maintained by the council to record sites threatened by redevelopment and to ensure that the losses to the city's heritage incurred during the 1960s are not repeated. Further manifestations of the desire to preserve the city's heritage were the revival of the medieval mystery plays and the midsummer watch parade.

By the 1970s development and slum clearance in the historic city, still only a small county borough, had further reduced its population. Most people lived in the expanding suburbs outside the borough's boundary. In 1974 the reorganisation of local government led to the creation of a two-tier system, with Chester becoming a district council. All the suburbs and considerable rural areas came under the council's control. In 1992, to mark the 40th anniversary of the Queen's accession, Chester's first citizen was allowed the honour of being termed Lord Mayor.

In the final quarter of the 20th century the city continued to grow and prosper. A southerly bypass road completed in 1977 to combat continuing traffic congestion then provided a new boundary for development on that side. A large business park was created to house financial services firms, which continue to form a major part of the local economy. Retail parks and supermarkets have relocated to the periphery of the suburbs where parking can be provided more easily and the city centre, with many streets now pedestrianised, still retains its major regional retailing status. The population decline in the historic centre has also been reversed. The brownfield sites left by the closure of the industrial concerns along the canal corridor have been redeveloped with apartment blocks. Chester has enjoyed very buoyant property prices that are significantly higher than the rest of North West England.

As the city moves into its third millennium, it is pledged to continue steering a course which combines a modern retail and service centre with respect for its historic heritage, both for its own sake and for the enjoyment of Cestrians, visitors and tourists alike.

151 *Urban regeneration: modern apartment blocks on the old Chester Leadworks site.*

Notes

Abbreviations

A.A.A.L.	*Annals of Archaeology and Anthropology of Liverpool*
J.C.A.S.	*Journal of the Chester Archaeological Society*
R.S.L.C.	*The Record Society for Lancashire and Cheshire*
V.C.H.	*Victoria History of the County of Chester*

Introduction

1. See, for example, Woodward, D., 'The port of Chester in context', in Carrington, P. (ed.), *Where Deva spreads her wizard stream* (1996), pp.61-5.
2. Dodgson, J. McN., *The Place-Names of Cheshire, pt V(I:i); the place names of the City of Chester* (1981), English Place-Name Society, pp.5-7.

1: Beginnings and the Arrival of the Romans

1. Garner, D. & Wilmott, A., 'Let the games begin', *British Archaeology*, no. 93 (2007), p.12.
2. Matthews, K., 'Iron Age sea-borne trade in Liverpool Bay', in Carrington (ed.), *Where Deva spreads her wizard stream*, pp.12-23.
3. Mason, D., *Excavations at Chester; the elliptical building: an image of the Roman world?* (2000).
4. Mason, D., *Excavations at Chester; the Roman fortress baths* (2005).
5. Mason, *Excavations at Chester; the elliptical building*, pp.76-80.
6. Petch, D.F., 'The Praetorium at Deva', *J.C.A.S.* vol.55 (1968), pp.1-6; Strickland, T. J., 'Chester: Excavations in the Princess Street / Hunter Street area 1978-1982. A first report on discoveries of the Roman period', *J.C.A.S.* vol.65 (1982), pp.5-24.

7. Mason, D., *Roman Chester: city of the eagles* (2001), pp.89-100.
8. Mason, D., *Excavations at Chester; 11-15 Castle Street* (1980).
9. Garner & Wilmott, 'Let the games begin', p.13.
10. Wright, R.P. & Richmond, I.A., *The Roman inscribed and sculptured stones in the Grosvenor Museum, Chester* (1955).

2: In Imperial Rome; the Legion and Civilians

1. Richmond, I.A. & Webster, G., 'Excavations at Goss Street, Chester, 1948-9', *J.C.A.S.* vol. 38 (1951), pp.1-38.
2. Petch, D.F., 'Excavations on the site of the Old Market Hall, Chester, second summary report 1968-70', *J.C.A.S.* vol.57 (1971), pp.13-15.
3. Strickland, T. J., 'The defences of Roman Chester: a note on discoveries made on the North Wall 1982', *J.C.A.S.* vol.65 (1982), pp.25-36.
4. Wright & Richmond, *The Roman inscribed and sculptured stones in the Grosvenor Museum, Chester*, p.17.
5. Ward, S. and Strickland, T. J., *Chester Excavations: Northgate Brewery 1974-5*, (1978).
6. Garner & Wilmott, 'Let the games begin', p.13.

7. Newstead, R., 'The Roman cemetery in the Infirmary Field, Chester', *A.A.A.L.* vol.6 (1914), pp.121-67.

8. Mason, D., *Excavations at Chester; 11-15 Castle Street*, pp.15-16.

9. Mason, D., 'And the walls came tumbling down: excavations adjacent to the City Walls in St John Street 1988/9', *J.C.A.S.* vol. 73 (1994/5), pp.11-20.

10. Garner & Wilmott, 'Let the games begin', p.15.

11. Henig, M., 'Chester and the Art of the Twentieth Legion', in Thacker, A.T., *Medieval Archaeology, Art and Archaeology at Chester* (Brit. Archaeol. Assoc. Conference Trans. Vol. 22, 2000), pp.1-15.

12. Mason, *Roman Chester: city of the eagles*, pp.188-91.

13. Mason, D., *The Heronbridge Research Project, second interim report* (2002), pp.41-7.

14. Newstead, R., 'Roman Chester: the extra-mural settlement at Saltney', *A.A.A.L.* vol.22, nos.1-2 (1935), pp.3-18.

15. Henig, M., 'Tales from the tomb', in Carrington, P. (ed.), *Deva Victrix; Roman Chester re-assessed* (2002), p. 75.

16. Hoffmann, B., 'Where have all the soldiers gone?' in Carrington (ed.), *Deva Victrix; Roman Chester re-assessed*, pp.80-2.

17. Mason, *Excavations at Chester; 11-15 Castle Street*, pp.18-21.

18. Mason, *Roman Chester: city of the eagles*, pp.199-204.

19. Malone, S.J., *Legio XX Valeria Victrix; prosopography, archaeology and history* (2006), pp.65-72.

3: Britons, Saxons and Vikings – Heroes, Legends and Saints

1. Bede, *A History of the English Church and People* (1970), p.103.

2. Mason, D., *The Heronbridge Research Project, third interim report* (2004).

3. Mason, D., *Chester AD 400-1066; from Roman fortress to English Town* (2007), pp.43-56.

4. Ward, S., *Excavations at Chester; Dark Age and Saxon occupation in the Roman fortress, sites excavated 1964-1981* (1994), p.116.

5. James, T.B., 'Medieval Britain and Ireland in 2005', *Medieval Archaeology* vol.50 (2006), p.302.

6. Matthews, K., *Excavations at Chester; the evolution of the heart of the city* (1995), pp.63-4.

7. Mason, *Excavations at Chester; the Roman fortress baths*, pp.83-4.

8. Cavill, P., Harding, S. & Jesch, J., *Wirral and its Viking heritage* (2000).

9. Matthews, S., 'Archbishop Plegmund and the court of King Alfred 890-923', *J.C.A.S.* vol.74 (1996-7), pp.89-114.

10. Matthews, K., *St Plegmund's Well: an archaeological and historical survey* (1995).

11. Ward, *Excavations at Chester; Dark Age and Saxon occupation in the Roman fortress*, p.117.

12. Mason, D., *Excavations at Chester; 26-42 Lower Bridge Street: the Dark Age and Saxon periods* (1985), pp.18-23.

13. Ward, S., *Excavations at Chester; 12 Watergate Street 1985; Roman Headquarters Building to Medieval Row* (1988), pp.29-31.

14. Ward, *Excavations at Chester; Dark Age and Saxon occupation in the Roman fortress*, p.66.

15. Ward, *Excavations at Chester; Dark Age and Saxon occupation in the Roman fortress*, pp.74-5.

16. Bu'Lock, J.D., *Pre-Conquest Cheshire 383-1066* (1972), p.55.

4: The Walled City

1. Barley, M.W., 'Town defences in England and Wales after 1066', in *The Plans and Topography of Medieval Towns in England and Wales* (1976).

2. Sawyer, P.H. and Thacker, A.T., 'Domesday Survey' in Harris, B.E. (ed.), *A History of the County of Cheshire, V.C.H.* vol.1 (1987), p.342.

3. Hill, D., 'The Burghal Hidage: the establishment of a text', *Medieval Archaeology* vol.13 (1969), pp.91-2.

4. Mason, D., 'And the walls came tumbling down', pp.11-20.

5. LeQuesne, C., *Excavations at Chester: The Roman and later defences*, Pt I (1999), pp.146-7.

6. Thompson, F.H., 'Excavations at Linenhall Street, Chester, 1961-2', *J.C.A.S.* vol.56 (1969), pp.11-14.

7. Thompson, 'Excavations at Linenhall Street, Chester, 1961-2', p.6.

8. Ward, S., *Chester City Ditches, a slice of history* (1992).

9. Lewis, C.P. & Thacker, A.T., *A History of the County of Chester; general history and topography*, V.C.H. vol.5, pt.1 (2003), p.17.

10. For more detail on the Norman earls see Husain, B.M.C., *Cheshire under the Norman Earls 1066-1237* (1973), pp.83-97.

11. Cather, S., Park, D. and Pender, R., 'Henry III's Wall Paintings at Chester Castle', in Thacker, A.T. (ed.) (2000), pp.170-89.

12. Donald Insall Associates Ltd, *Chester Castle Conservation Plan* (2001), pp.10-20.

13. Alldridge, N.J., 'The topography of early medieval Chester', *J.C.A.S.* vol.64 (1981), pp.5-31.

14. Renn, D., 'The Water Tower at Chester', *J.C.A.S.* vol.45 (1958), p.57.

15. Alebon, P.H., Davey, P.J. and Robinson, D.J., 'The Eastgate, Chester, 1972', *J.C.A.S.* vol.59 (1976), pp.37-49.

16. J. Laughton, unpublished report.

17. Unpublished excavation, but see Ward, *Chester City Ditches, a slice of history.*

18. Christie, R.C., 'Annales Cestrienses or Chronicle of the Abbey of St Werburgh, at Chester', *R.S.L.C.* vol.14 (1886), pp.87-9.

19. Colvin, H.M., *The History of the King's Works* (1963) vol.1, p.183.

20. Donald Insall Associates Ltd., *Chester Castle Conservation Plan*, p.10.

21. Colvin, *The History of the King's Works*, pp.393, 468.

22. Lewis & Thacker, *A History of the County of Chester; general history and topography*, p.211.

23. Madison, J.M., 'The Choir of Chester Cathedral', *J.C.A.S.* vol.66 (1983), pp.31-46.

24. Turner, R.C., Sale, C.B. and Axworthy Rutter, J.A., 'A medieval garden at the Belgrave Moat, Cheshire', *J.C.A.S.* vol.69 (1988), pp.59-78.

25. Lewis & Thacker, *A History of the County of Chester; general history and topography*, p.56.

5: The Medieval City – Trade and Clerics

1. Lewis & Thacker, *A History of the County of Chester; general history and topography*, p.24.

2. Ward, S., 'The archaeology of medieval Chester: a review', *J.C.A.S.* vol.73 (1994/5), pp.56-7.

3. Taylor, M.V., 'Liber Luciani de laude Cestrie', *R.S.L.C.* vol.64 (1912), pp.46, 58, 65.

4. Ward, *Excavations at Chester; 12 Watergate Street* 1985, pp.46-52.

5. Hawkins, E. (ed.), 'Henry Bradshaw: Life of St Werburgh', *Chetham Soc.* vol.15 (1848), pp.194-7.

6. Christie, 'Annales Cestrienses or Chronicle of the Abbey of St Werburgh, at Chester', p.105.

7. Bennett, J.H.E., 'The Black Friars of Chester', *J.C.A.S.* vol.39 (1952), pp.30-1.

8. Bennett, J.H.E., 'The Grey Friars of Chester', *J.C.A.S.* vol.24, pt.1 (1921), pp.11-15.

9. Lewis, C.P. & Thacker, A.T., *A History of the County of Chester; general history and topography*, V.C.H. vol.5, pt. 2 (2005), p.244.

10. Tait, J., 'Chartulary or Register of the Abbey of St Werburgh, Chester, Pt II', *Chetham Soc.* vol.82 (1923), pp.301-2.

11. Ward, S., *Excavations at Chester; the lesser medieval religious houses, sites investigated 1964-1983* (1990).

12. Garner, D., *Report on an archaeological evaluation at Linenhall Stables, Stanley Street, Chester* (2002).

13. Lewis & Thacker, *A History of the County of Chester; general history and topography*, p.106.

14. Brown, A. (ed.), *The Rows of Chester; the Chester Rows Research Project* (1999), p.63.

15. Bennett, 'The Black Friars of Chester', p.47.

16. Cracknell, B., *Outrageous Waves: global warming and coastal change in Britain through two thousand years* (2005), pp.1-9.

17. Bennett, 'The Grey Friars of Chester', p.29.

18. Ward, *Excavations at Chester; the lesser medieval religious houses*, pp.37-9.

19. Brown, *The Rows of Chester*, pp.63-4.

6: County Town and Civil Strife – the Sixteenth and Seventeenth Centuries

1. Beck, J., *Tudor Cheshire* (1969), p.8.
2. Langtree, S. & Comyns, A. (eds.), *2000 Years of Building – Chester's architectural legacy* (2001), pp.96-7.
3. Davey, P., *The archaeology of the clay tobacco pipe 3: Britain, the north and west* (1980).
4. Burne, R.V.H., *Chester Cathedral* (1958), pp.30-2.
5. Burne, *Chester Cathedral*, pp.9-13.
6. Bennett, J.H.E., 'The White Friars of Chester', *J.C.A.S.* vol.31, pt.1 (1935), p. 44.
7. For a detailed discussion and description of the Civil War defences see Ward, S., *Excavations at Chester; the Civil War Siegeworks 1642-1646* (1987).
8. Ward, *Excavations at Chester; the Civil War Siegeworks 1642-1646*, p.7.
9. Barratt, J., *The Great Siege of Chester* (2003), pp.43-4.
10. Ward, *Excavations at Chester; the Civil War Siegeworks 1642-1646*, p.11.
11. Malbon, T., 'Memorials of the Civil War in Cheshire', in Hall, J. (ed.), *R.S.L.C.* vol. 65 (1889), p.157.
12. Barratt, *The Great Siege of Chester*, pp.93-106.
13. Ward, *Excavations at Chester; the Civil War Siegeworks 1642-1646*, pp.32-7.
14. Harleian MS. 2155, reprinted in Morris, R.H., 'The siege of Chester, 1643-1646', *J.C.A.S.* vol.25 (1923), pp.215-36.
15. Barratt, *The Great Siege of Chester*, pp.157-65.
16. Dore, R.N., 'The letter books of Sir William Brereton, Vol. II'. *R.S.L.C.* vol.128 (1990), pp.82-3.
17. For Randle Holme's detailed account of the damage see Morris R.H., 'The siege of Chester, 1643-1646', pp. 203-5.
18. Malbon, 'Memorials of the Civil War in Cheshire', pp.222-3.
19. Dore, R.N., *The Civil Wars in Cheshire* (1966), p.93.

7: Polite Society

1. Dore, *The Civil Wars in Cheshire*, pp.89-95, and Ormerod, G., *History of Cheshire* (2nd edition, ed. T. Helsby) vol.1 (1882), pp.525-35.
2. Burne, *Chester Cathedral*, pp.152-3.
3. Donald Insall Associates Ltd, *Chester Castle Conservation Plan*.
4. Brown, A. (ed.), *The Rows of Chester; the Chester Rows Research Project*, p.168.
5. Brown, *The Rows of Chester; the Chester Rows Research Project*, p.183-4.
6. Langtree, S. & Comyns, A. (eds), *2000 Years of Building – Chester's architectural legacy* (2001), p.66.
7. Brown, A. (ed.), *The Rows of Chester; the Chester Rows Research Project*, p. 113.
8. Langtree, S. & Comyns, A. (eds), *2000 Years of Building – Chester's architectural legacy*, p.107.
9. Langtree, S. & Comyns, A. (eds), *2000 Years of Building – Chester's architectural legacy*, pp.130-1.
10. Baskerville, S.W., 'The establishment of the Grosvenor interest in Chester, 1710-48', *J.C.A.S.* vol.63 (1980), pp.59-84.
11. Donald Insall Associates Ltd, *Chester Castle Conservation Plan*, p.26.
12. Pevsner, N. & Hubbard, E., *The buildings of England: Cheshire* (1971), p.175.
13. Donald Insall Associates Ltd, *Chester Castle Conservation Plan* (2001), p.36.
14. Burne, R.V.H., *Chester Cathedral*, p.200.
15. Kennett, A.M., *Chester and the River Dee* (1982), pp.10-11.
16. Barnes J.K., 'New bridge, new road, new church, the building of Grosvenor Street in Chester', *J.C.A.S.* vol.76 (2000-1). pp.43-55.
17. Clarke, J.W., 'The building of Grosvenor Bridge', *J.C.A.S.* vol. 45 (1958), pp.43-55.

8: Industry, Workers and Shoppers

1. Langtree & Comyns (eds), *2000 Years of Building – Chester's architectural legacy*, p.147.
2. Herson J., 'Victorian Chester: a city of change and ambiguity', in Swift, R. (ed.), *Victorian Chester* (1996), pp.17-18.
3. Carrington, P., *English Heritage Book of Chester* (1994), p.97.

4. Herson, J., 'Canals, railways and the demise of the port of Chester', in Carrington (ed.), *Where Deva spreads her wizard stream*, pp.75-89.

5. Herson, 'Canals, railways and the demise of the port of Chester', p.83.

6. Dixon, J. & Pickard, G., *Railways around Saltney, a pictorial record* (2006) pp.150-2.

7. Jansen, V., 'George Gilbert Scott and Restoration at Chester Cathedral, 1819-1876', in Thacker (ed.) (2000), pp.81-98.

8. Barrow, J.S., 'Public Utilities', in Lewis & Thacker, *A History of the County of Chester; general history and topography*, pp.37-9.

9. Herson, 'Victorian Chester: a city of change and ambiguity', p.19.

10. Wilding, R., *Miller of Dee* (1997).

11. Lewis, C., 'Chester Races', in Lewis & Thacker, *A History of the County of Chester; general history and topography*, pp.258-9.

12. Jeffes, K., 'The Irish in early Victorian Chester: an outcast community?', in Swift (ed.), *Victorian Chester*.

13. Reed-Purvis, J., 'Black Sunday: skeleton army disturbances in late Victorian Chester', in Swift (ed.), *Victorian Chester*, pp.185-206.

14. Durdy, R., 'The Fenians in Chester, 1867', *Cheshire History* vol. 46 (2006-7), pp.104-18.

15. Wilding, *Miller of Dee*, p.35.

9: Modern Chester – the City lost and found

1. The development of the city described in this chapter draws heavily on Lewis, C.P. & Thacker, A.T., *A History of the County of Chester; general history and topography*, V.C.H., vol.5, pt.1 (2003), pp.239-72.

2. Lewis & Thacker, *A History of the County of Chester; general history and topography*, p.235.

3. Langtree & Comyns (eds), *2000 Years of Building – Chester's architectural legacy*, pp.188-9.

4. Langtree & Comyns (eds), *2000 Years of Building – Chester's architectural legacy*, p.191.

5. Ellis, J.E.H., *From the Boyne to Basra; a short history of the 22nd (Cheshire) Regiment* (2007), pp.77-101.

6. Lewis & Thacker, *A History of the County of Chester; general history and topography*, pp.240-1.

7. Bruce, J.A., 'Giles Gilbert Scott and the Chester war memorial project', *J.C.A.S.* vol. 73 (1994/5), pp.99-114.

8. Lewis & Thacker, *A History of the County of Chester; general history and topography*, pp.243-5.

9. Barfield, N., *Broughton: from Wellington to Airbus* (2001), p.9.

10. Stuart, E. (ed.), *What did you do in the War Deva?* (2005).

11. Ellis, *From the Boyne to Basra; a short history of the 22nd (Cheshire) Regiment*, pp.111-39.

12. Stuart, *What did you do in the War Deva?*, pp.75-7.

13. Barfield, *Broughton: from Wellington to Airbus*, p.35.

14. Stuart, *What did you do in the War Deva?*, pp.67-9.

15. Stuart, *What did you do in the War Deva?*, pp.133-68.

16. Barfield, *Broughton: from Wellington to Airbus*, pp.65, 111.

17. Wilding, *Miller of Dee*, p.17.

18. Barfield, *Broughton: from Wellington to Airbus*, p. 91.

19. Mason, *Excavations at Chester; the elliptical building*, pp.4-6; Mason, *Excavations at Chester; the Roman fortress baths*, pp.3-4.

20. Donald Insall Associates Ltd, *Chester; a study in conservation*.

21. Thompson, *The excavation of the Roman amphitheatre at Chester*.

Bibliography

Barfield, N., *Broughton: from Wellington to Airbus* (2001)

Barratt, J., *The Great Siege of Chester* (2003)

Beck, J., *Tudor Cheshire* (1969)

Brown, A. (ed.), *The Rows of Chester; the Chester Rows Research Project* (1999)

Burne, R.V.H., *Chester Cathedral* (1958)

Bu'Lock, J.D., *Pre-Conquest Cheshire 383-1066* (1972)

Carrington, P. (ed.), *Deva Victrix: Roman Chester Re-assessed* (Chester Archaeological Society, 2002)

Carrington, P. (ed.), *Where Deva spreads her wizard stream* (1996)

Carrington, P., *English Heritage Book of Chester* (1994)

Cavill, P., Harding, S. & Jesch, J., *Wirral and its Viking heritage* (2000)

Colvin, H.M., *The History of the King's Works* (1963)

Dixon, J. & Pickard, G., *Railways around Saltney, a pictorial record* (2006)

Dodgson, J. McN., *The Place-Names of Cheshire, pt V(I:i); the place names of the City of Chester* (1981)

Donald Insall Associates Ltd, *Chester; a study in conservation* (1968)

Donald Insall Associates Ltd, *Chester Castle Conservation Plan* (2001)

Dore, R.N., *The Civil Wars in Cheshire* (1966)

Ellis, J.E.H., *From the Boyne to Basra; a short history of the 22nd (Cheshire) Regiment* (2007)

Harris, B.E. (ed.), *A History of the County of Cheshire, V.C.H. vol.1* (1987)

Hodson, J.H., *Cheshire, 1660-1780: Restoration to Industrial Revolution* (1978)

Husain, B.M.C., *Cheshire under the Norman Earls 1066-1237* (1973)

Kennett, A.M., *Chester and the River Dee* (1982)

Langtree, S. & Comyns, A. (eds), *2000 Years of Building – Chester's architectural legacy* (2001)

LeQuesne, C., *Excavations at Chester: The Roman and later defences, Pt I* (1999)

Lewis, C.P. & Thacker, A.T., *A History of the County of Chester; general history and topography, V.C.H. vol.5, pt.1* (2003); pt. 2 (2005)

Malone, S.J., *Legio XX Valeria Victrix; prosopography, archaeology and history* (2006)

Mason, D., *Excavations at Chester; the elliptical building: an image of the Roman world?* (2000)

Mason, D., *Roman Chester: city of the eagles* (2001)

Mason, D., *Excavations at Chester; the Roman fortress baths* (2005)

Mason, D., *Chester AD 400-1066; from Roman fortress to English Town* (2007)

Matthews, K., *Excavations at Chester; the evolution of the heart of the city* (1995)

Matthews, K., *St Plegmund's Well: an archaeological and historical survey* (1995)

Ormerod, G., *History of Cheshire* (2nd edition, ed. T. Helsby) vol.1 (1882), pp.525-35

Pevsner, N. & Hubbard, E., *The buildings of England: Cheshire* (1971)

Stuart, E. (ed.), *What did you do in the War Deva?* (2005)

Thacker, A.T., *Medieval Archaeology, Art and Archaeology at Chester* (Brit. Archaeol. Assoc. Conference Trans. Vol. 22, 2000)

Thompson, F.H., *The excavation of the Roman amphitheatre at Chester* (1976)

Ward, S., *Excavations at Chester; the Civil War Siegeworks 1642-1646* (1987)

Ward, S., *Excavations at Chester; 12 Watergate Street 1985; Roman Headquarters Building to Medieval Row* (1988)

Ward, S., *Excavations at Chester; the lesser medieval religious houses, sites investigated 1964-1983* (1990)

Ward, S., *Chester City Ditches, a slice of history* (1992)

Ward, S., *Excavations at Chester; Dark Age and Saxon occupation in the Roman fortress, sites excavated 1964-1981* (1994)

Wilding, R., *Miller of Dee* (1997)

Wright, R.P. & Richmond, I.A., *The Roman inscribed and sculptured stones in the Grosvenor Museum, Chester* (1955)

Index

References which relate to illustrations only are given in **bold**.